We live in a world today where people are hurting desperately. People are starving for answers to the deepest issues of life—and man's answers are simply not capable of meeting the needs.

Where do the answers lie? They can be found in only one source: in the clear revelation of God's Word.

I believe it's the Lord's desire to prepare His people to be channels of His love to hurting people—to be compassionate, loving vessels, equipped to share His Word.

People are looking for help, and Christians are being called upon more and more to give help and advice—to their friends, neighbors, co-workers, and children.

Where else can people go when faced with the heartache of divorce, drug problems, child abuse, and other sufferings? When they cry out to God for answers, who will be there to meet their needs?

We can be there, to bring His healing love to bind the wounds.

This is why this handbook is so important. I am persuaded that as you allow this book to minister deeply to your own needs, God will nourish you and enable you to become a great blessing to others.

Whether you have problems in your marriage, your personal life, or with your children—you will discover the Lord as your infallible resource, even as this book leads you into the riches of His Word.

May God bless you as you begin to feast upon His answers—and as you share them with others. May He bring you into ever more abundant life, and make you a help to everyone around you.

PAT ROBERTSON

THE
CBN
MINISTRY
HANDBOOK

Biblical Solutions
for Everyday Problems

CBN PARTNERS EDITION

Tyndale House Publishers, Inc.
Wheaton, Illinois

CONTENTS

PREFACE

Problems. Everyone has them.

Our CBN telephone counselors hear daily from thousands of hurting people who call our toll-free number to ask questions and to share almost every human problem imaginable: alcoholism, fear, homosexuality, envy, divorce. Our counselors listen. Share God's Word. Pray.

Then, if asked, they send practical, biblically based pamphlets to further help the person who has called.

Time and again, that literature has been just what was needed to help suffering people find solutions to their problems. Those who have received such literature call and write us constantly to tell of miracles which have occurred as a result of applying the sound biblical counsel contained in them.

This is why, for the first time, we have assembled these pamphlets in the book you hold in your hands—*The CBN Ministry Handbook.*

In *The CBN Ministry Handbook,* you will find God's answers to some of the most pressing issues facing people today, including remarriage, incest/molestation, freedom from demon bondage, and anger. The handbook contains countless Scripture references to aid you in both your study and personal application of God's Word, as well as special teaching topics such as "The Full Counsel of God."

You can use *The CBN Ministry Handbook,* along with the Bible, as you seek to minister God's compassion and hope to those around you. And, as you do, we're certain you'll be helped as well. That's because *The CBN Ministry Handbook* is not *just* a counseling tool—it is for your own use as well. Its personal, practical approach will assist you as you seek God's wisdom for solutions to the problems, needs, and questions you face from day to day.

God's love and grace abounds toward those who sincerely seek *His* wisdom, *His* answers. He cares about your problems, and we

PREFACE

at CBN care too. If you need additional support or prayer, please don't hesitate to call our toll-free number (1-800-446-0700) or contact your nearest CBN Counseling Center. We'd love to help you—and see you help others as well!

THE EDITORS

INTRODUCTION

How to Use This Handbook for Yourself

Using this handbook for your own personal growth is the best place to start. No matter what problems you may face, you will discover scriptural answers to them within these pages. Naturally, not all problems in life can be solved immediately. But there is something you can receive immediately—the blessing of knowing what God has to say about your particular situation.

Jesus Christ is concerned about every detail of your life, no matter how small or large. It is not surprising, then, to find that the Bible is filled with answers to every conceivable problem you may have to deal with in life.

Take just a few moments to look over the topics that are discussed in this handbook. Then turn to those sections that deal with the problems you face most often, and find out what the Bible has to say on those subjects. Next, memorize the Scriptures given to help you with those problems.

As God's Word is richly planted within your heart, you will find the wisdom and insight needed to deal with the problem, whatever it may be. And as you begin to memorize Bible passages, you will find that not only will you help yourself—but you will also help others as you share the truth of God's Word with them in time of need.

How to Use This Handbook to Help Others

This handbook deals with some of the most common problems people face today. As a person shares his particular problem with you, you will probably sense which topic you should turn to in the handbook for solutions. If counseling by telephone, you may want to share with the person straight from the handbook. If ministering face to face, however, you may want to just listen to the problem first, then refer to the book later and follow through with counsel at another time.

9

INTRODUCTION

Here are some general steps you may want to follow when counseling:

1. Stop, look, and listen to the person you are trying to help.

2. Identify the main problem. It is important to pray, either silently or with the other person, for God's wisdom in this.

3. Share Scripture and counsel.

4. Ask for a response.

5. Follow through with prayer and ministry as the need is discerned.

6. Give homework and refer the person to a pastor if needed.

As a Christian counselor, you are a comfort to those who are suffering and a helper to those in need. Your role should not be to debate theological matters, but to listen compassionately and to help ease the burden of the other person by praying and sharing God's Word.

Remember to allow Scripture to be your guide while counseling. God's Word is powerful, and along with God-given wisdom, common sense, and the guidance of the Holy Spirit, you will find yourself "competent to counsel."

Counseling Principles

DO:

1. Pray without ceasing. Give thanks and praise to God in all circumstances.

2. Listen prayerfully. Anticipate the Holy Spirit's guidance in what you are to do, speak, or pray for. (It may or may not be what the person requested.)

3. Quote Bible passages that speak directly to the problem. Include both those that analyze it and those that will give the person direction in overcoming it.

4. Be courteous and helpful. Recognize that the person is hoping that you will be able to help.

5. Speak and act with the authority that Christ gives to us. Resist Satan. Speak directly to the problem, rather than about it or around it.

6. Keep any commitments you may make to the person, such as promising to pray or providing additional assistance.

7. Share the principles of agreement, fasting, praise, favor, giving, and intercession that are found in this handbook. Encourage the person to learn and to practice them.

8. Be a channel of God's love always. Love often triumphs when all else fails.

9. Expect God to answer your prayers supernaturally as a result of the gifts of the Holy Spirit in operation.

DO NOT:

1. Do not argue, condemn, criticize, preach, "talk down to," or overreact to the person by talking loudly.

2. Never counsel someone to leave their church or to change from one church to another (unless the person is involved in the occult or a non-Christian religious group).

3. Do not counsel someone to stop taking medication or to neglect seeing a doctor. These are decisions you cannot make.

4. Never counsel someone to get a divorce or to leave a spouse, or to do anything else that is contrary to Scripture.

5. You should not dictate what the person is to do—you should only suggest. The decision must be made by the person himself.

INTRODUCTION

In Summary

The solutions found within the pages of this handbook have been a source of comfort and strength for countless thousands—because they are *God's* solutions. They are His answers for the needs of a hurting world. May He use this special handbook to draw both you and your loved ones closer to Him, and to make you even more aware of His boundless love and concern for you.

Notes

_____

_____

_____

_____

_____

_____

_____

_____

_____

ABORTION

The Bible states, "Thou shalt not kill [murder]." Since the Bible also states that children are God's heritage and His reward, it is wrong to take the life of an unborn child. As the following Scriptures show, the giving and taking of life is God's prerogative.

"Thou shalt not kill" (Deuteronomy 5:17).

"Lo, children are an heritage of the Lord: and the fruit of the womb is his reward" (Psalm 127:3).

"He maketh the barren woman to keep house, and to be a joyful mother of children. Praise ye the Lord" (Psalm 113:9).

Yet there is a great turmoil surrounding the very real problem of what to do with an unwanted pregnancy. You may be ashamed because the child you are carrying is illegitimate. Or maybe you have no desire for a child and the financial and emotional burdens it would entail. Or perhaps you already have had an abortion and now feel guilty about it.

If You Are Considering an Abortion . . .

Abortion is not an option. It is murder. But don't despair, God is in charge. There are no hopeless situations with Him.

Have your baby. God will redeem the situation, just as He did for Joseph. Joseph's brothers meant to kill him, but God preserved him and used the sequence of events to save an entire people. As Joseph remarked to his brothers, "And God sent me before you to preserve you a posterity in the earth, and to save your lives by a great deliverance" (Genesis 45:7).

Perhaps you are carrying a child from an illegitimate union. Many of us have family members—even spouses—who would not be alive today if illegitimate, unwanted children had been aborted. The life within you is a precious gift from God. Don't kill it.

ABORTION

If You Have Had an Abortion . . .

If you have had an abortion, you may feel burdened with the guilt of having taken a life. But you may be encouraged by the fact that some of the greatest biblical heroes were guilty of having taken lives. Paul consented to the murder of Stephen, yet after his conversion became the apostle to the Gentiles. Moses and King David were also murderers. Yet they repented, as did Paul, and God forgave them. In fact, they became the greatest of God's men ever known. For although God despises murder just as He does any sin, He loved these men. And He loves you too. If you repent and confess your sin to Him, He will forgive you and cleanse you of it (1 John 1:9). Then go and sin no more (Isaiah 55:7). God has a great love for you, even now. The Bible says that in Christ, old things (sins) pass away. All things become new. Your sins will not be remembered by God once you have truly repented and turned your life over to Christ (Isaiah 43:25).

Then What?

Call on Jesus, confessing your sin, and receive Him as your Savior and Lord (Romans 10:13; 1 John 1:9; John 1:12).

Ask Jesus to baptize you with the Holy Spirit (Luke 11:13). You will receive the ability you need to begin living a victorious, happy life (Ephesians 6:10-18). Then, as you begin to help other people through your life and testimony, you will discover a new fulfillment and unspeakable joy of living for others instead of yourself.

Finally, be encouraged to talk to your minister. You may also wish to contact an unwed mothers' group if available. Be sure to seek out and attend a Bible-believing church regularly.

As You Pray

Pray for God's grace and courage to face all that you must face. Praise and thank God that we are not dealt with according to our transgressions. Thank Him for accepting and forgiving you. And thank Him for giving you grace to forgive yourself and anyone else who may be involved in the situation, such as the child's father.

References/Homework

Read the story of Joseph in Genesis and of King David in 2 Samuel 11, 12.

Psalm 139:13-16	God knows a person from conception
Proverbs 31	Ideal woman and mother
Matthew 6:33	Seek God first
3 John 2	You will prosper as your soul does spiritually
Romans 8:31	Whom God is for, who can be against?
Philippians 3:13, 14; 4:13	Forget the past
Isaiah 40:31	Promised strength to carry on
Isaiah 44:2	Formed from the womb
Jeremiah 1:5	Known by God before conception

Notes

_____

_____

_____

_____

_____

_____

_____

_____

_____

THE PRINCIPLE
OF AGREEMENT

The principle of agreement is that "the place of agreement is the place of power." It is a basic key to the Kingdom of God. There is great power in agreeing with God, His Word, and other Christians.

In fact, our salvation is based on a covenant or "agreement" God made with us. Through Jesus' atonement for our sins, God has made a way to bring us into agreement with Him. Because of this, He can show us favor.

God has promised us that if we are in agreement with Him, abiding in Him and His Word, then He will hear and answer us when we pray. Furthermore, when any two believers agree on any one thing and pray according to God's will, He has promised to answer (Matthew 18:19).

Belief brings agreement with God and is manifested in obedience to Him. Unbelief causes disagreement and disobedience. Disagreement results in division, discord, and rebellion. It also causes double-mindedness. A double-minded person should not expect to have his prayers answered (James 1:6, 8).

The principle of agreement is powerful not only in the Kingdom of God, but in the secular world as well. It applies to all interpersonal relationships, including marriage, family, and employment situations.

What Scripture Says

"And when the day of Pentecost was fully come, they were all with *one accord* in one place" (Acts 2:1).

"And when they heard that they lifted up their voice to God with *one accord,* and said, Lord, thou art God, which has made heaven, and earth, and the sea, and all that in them is. And when they had prayed, the place was shaken where they were assembled together;

and they were all filled with the Holy Ghost, and they spake the word of God with boldness" (Acts 4:24, 31).

"Peter therefore was kept in prison: But prayer was made without ceasing *of the church* unto God for him" (Acts 12:5).

"Again I say unto you, that *if two of you shall agree* on earth as touching anything that they shall ask, it shall be done for them of my Father which is in heaven" (Matthew 18:19).

Agree As You Pray
Especially as you pray, agree with God and expect that He is answering your prayer. Agree with another person concerning your prayer. God said He would answer.

The Kingdom of God vs. the Realm of Satan
"Who hath delivered us from the power of darkness, and hath translated us into the kingdom of his dear Son" (Colossians 1:13).

Everything in the Kingdom of God is positive. Everything in the realm of Satan is negative. Take an honest self-inventory. Are you positive or negative? Do you appreciate and build up your family members, friends, and fellow workers by being positive and agreeable, or do you drag them down by being negative, critical, and disagreeable?

Begin to show praise, appreciation and agreement in all your interpersonal relationships. Do the same with God. He said He honors those who honor Him (1 Samuel 2:30b). In like manner, you will begin to see a positive response in the people you associate with, especially those closest to you.

You will find yourself loving your fellowman. You will discover the brightness of God's world.

References/Homework
2 Kings 5:14	Naaman's healing
2 Samuel 12:13	David blessed
Jonah 3:3	Jonah's agreement

ALCOHOL/ ALCOHOLISM

An alcoholic can't control his drinking. If you are an alcoholic, you have a compulsive desire to drink. When you drink, your negative personality traits, such as anger, may be intensified and your problems may seem magnified. In order to cover up your alcoholism, you may tend to overdo in other areas of your life. Chances are, you need a drink at certain times of the day in order to get going to face your problems or to relax. And you may even drink on the job. Of course this means that your work and efficiency are slacking off. And your home life is probably suffering as well. You are enslaved by the sin of alcoholism.

Yet there is hope. God is able to deliver you completely by cleansing, sanctifying, and justifying you (1 Corinthians 6:9-11). Though alcohol abuse is a failing of the flesh (Galatians 5:19-21), the Holy Spirit can and will produce the self-control you need to overcome it (Galatians 5:22, 23).

What Scripture Says

"He that covereth his sins shall not prosper: but whoso *confesseth and forsaketh* them shall have mercy" (Proverbs 28:13).

"If we say that we have no sin, we deceive ourselves, and the truth is not in us. If we confess our sins, he is faithful and just to forgive us our sins, and to *cleanse* us from all unrighteousness" (1 John 1:8, 9).

"*Thine own* wickedness shall correct thee, and thy backslidings shall reprove thee: know therefore and see that it is an evil thing and bitter, that thou hast forsaken the Lord thy God, and that my fear is not in thee, saith the Lord God of hosts" (Jeremiah 2:19).

"For God sent not his Son into the world *to condemn* the world;

18

but that the world through him might be saved" (John 3:17).

"Jesus answered and said unto her: If thou knewest the gift of God, and who it is that saith to thee, Give me to drink; thou wouldest have asked of him, and he would have given thee living water" (John 4:10).

"But ye shall *receive power after* that the Holy Ghost is come upon you: and ye shall be witnesses unto me both in Jerusalem, and in all Judea, and in Samaria, and unto the uttermost part of the earth" (Acts 1:8). (Here is the key to beating alcoholism—through the power to overcome.)

"But the fruit of the Spirit is love, joy, peace, long-suffering, gentleness, goodness, faith [faithfulness], meekness, *temperance* [will power], against such there is no law" (Galatians 5:22, 23). (God will produce willpower for the powerless.)

Is There Hope?

If you have a drinking problem, you have probably felt condemned by yourself and others. Rather than condemning, however, God emphasizes how to overcome by receiving salvation, the baptism of the Holy Spirit, and the fruit of the Spirit. With these you will have the ability to become free and stay free of alcohol.

The saying "once an alcoholic, always an alcoholic" is based on the fact that a recovered alcoholic can never go back to drinking in any amount without being controlled by it again. Therefore, you need to ask God to deliver you from the desire to drink at all.

Practical Help

You probably have tried to stop drinking before and it has not worked for you. You may have tried religion or you may even be a Christian. What you need is practical spiritual help. Seek out a Spirit-filled counselor. Ask him to pray for deliverance for you—especially from compulsiveness, psychological and physical dependence, and even from the *desire* to drink.

You may have been told, "You must stop drinking and never drink again." But the pressure of having to face life without drinking may be overwhelming. Focus on the present. Decide that you will not have a drink *right now*. Live one day at a time.

You need to modify your lifestyle. The Bible speaks of being "transformed by the renewing of your mind" (Romans 12:2). You can renew your mind through your reading and thinking habits. The Bible and devotional testimonial books will be most helpful. Dwell on God and His Word rather than on your problem.

Learn and follow the principle of praise (honor and respect) to God each time you are tempted to drink. "By him therefore let us offer the sacrifice of praise to God continually . . . giving thanks to his name" (Hebrews 13:15). It is important to change your perspective from yourself to God and from the drink to God. Praise God the Problem Solver rather than the problem. Remember that you can be just as chained to sin by trying not to do it as you are by doing it. Because as long as your attention is on the sin, you are honoring it. But if your attention is on God, you are honoring Him. "Looking unto Jesus the author and finisher of our faith" (Hebrews 12:2a).

Contact a Spirit-filled church or prayer group and Alcoholics Anonymous. A local church pastor can help you do this.

Your close relatives may need to know how to help spiritually in your effort to recover. They should know that openly condemning an alcoholic is not effective. It may just feed your sense of "joyous agony" because you are "getting what you deserve." Jesus came to save, not condemn (John 3:17).

That's not to say that they should tolerate your alcoholic behavior. Instead, they should offer to help you. Your spouse, friends, or relatives can find out how to help you by contacting a Spirit-filled fellowship, Alcoholics Anonymous, or ALANON, an organization for friends and relatives of alcoholics.

As You Pray

If you are not yet a born-again Christian, ask God to forgive you, save you, and fill you with the Holy Spirit. An unforgiven, uncleansed drunkard cannot inherit the Kingdom of God (1 Corinthians 6:10; 1 John 1:8, 9; Romans 10:13; Luke 13:5; Acts 1:8).

Pray for deliverance. Offer thanks and praise for God's deliverance, mercy, ever-present help and power to overcome.

Pray for deliverance from fear—the fear that "I won't be able to make it" (2 Timothy 1:7).

References/Homework

2 Timothy 2:1, 4, 5, 11-13	Boldness, courage, God's faithfulness
Philippians 3:12-14	Forget the past
Psalm 103:12	Separation from sin
Isaiah 40:31	Strength renewed
John 8:36	Free in Jesus
Galatians 5:1	Freedom assured
Galatians 5:22, 23	Fruit of the Spirit
Romans 10:17	Faith imparted
Romans 8:31-37	Assurance in Christ
Proverbs 29:25	Safety in Jesus

Using a Bible concordance, study every reference for "fear," "deliverance," "healing," and "praise."

Practice "agreeing with God" about His promises for you and "disagreeing with Satan," who tries to accuse you to yourself, to God, to your family, friends, employers, etc.

Seek out other reformed drinkers. Look for their support.

Read *The Drinking Game, and How to Beat It,* Author Anonymous, Benco Edition, available from the Benjamin Company, 485 Madison Avenue, New York, New York 10022.

What to do the first day without a drink
1. Clean up, dress up.
2. Try to eat something.
3. Don't exaggerate any discomfort.
4. Avoid arguments and other conflicts.
5. Do things you can easily do.
6. Face your social situation realistically.
7. Stay away from your drinking buddies.

8. Know that you are not alone. Many other people are going through what you are today.
9. Don't waste time worrying about whether you will sleep tonight.

The next few days
1. Remember, God loves you. Sin has no claim upon you.
2. Be prepared to refuse a drink.
3. Don't rationalize that: (a) I need a drink to keep going or (b) the bad times are to be blamed for my being underfed or overly tired.
4. Reaffirm, "I'm not going to have a drink *today!*"
5. Remember Philippians 4:13, "I can do all things through Christ which strengtheneth me."

Notes

_____

_____

_____

_____

_____

_____

_____

_____

_____

ANGER

Anger, if not recognized as a sin and repented of, will eventually express itself hurtfully toward others.

The Bible tells us that the anger of man does not achieve the righteousness of God (James 1:19-21).

What Scripture Says

"Cease from anger, and forsake wrath: Fret not thyself in any wise to do evil" (Psalm 37:8).

"Let all bitterness, and wrath, and anger, and clamour, and evil speaking, be put away from you, with all malice" (Ephesians 4:31).

"But now ye also put off all these: anger, wrath, malice, blasphemy, filthy communication out of your mouth" (Colossians 3:8).

"An angry man stirreth up strife, and a furious man aboundeth in transgression" (Proverbs 29:22).

"Be not hasty in thy spirit to be angry: For anger resteth in the bosom of fools" (Ecclesiastes 7:9).

How to Overcome

When anger is manifested in your life, totally yielding to the Holy Spirit will replace the anger with God's love regardless of the circumstances you may encounter.

This is consistent with God's Word, in which we are told to love our enemies who hate, curse, and abuse us by blessing them and praying for them (Luke 6:27, 28).

Jesus, as He hung dying on the cross at Calvary, had every right to be angry toward those who placed Him there, and yet He asked His Father to forgive them. Through this supreme sacrifice of love, all of those who believe and call upon His name shall be saved (completed).

By our godly responses toward others we too can be a part of the

ANGER

Holy Spirit's work in convicting and completing God's work in them. The following guidelines will assist you in overcoming anger.

1. Recognize anger as sin
   "Put away anger and forgive" (Ephesians 4:30-32).
2. Confess it as sin
   "If we confess our sins, He is faithful to forgive" (1 John 1:9).
3. Receive God's release
   "If we ask anything according to His will He hears and answers" (1 John 5:14, 15)
4. Ask God to fill you with His Holy Spirit
   "Your Heavenly Father will give the Holy Spirit to those who ask" (Luke 11:13).

As You Pray

Ask God to forgive you for your anger and give you His love for them. Ask those with whom you are angry to forgive you and thank God for the victory over anger.

References/Homework

Read *Spirit-Controlled Temperament,* Tim LaHaye, Tyndale House Publishers, Inc.

Proverbs 14:17	He that is angry does foolishly
Proverbs 14:29	He that is hasty of spirit exalteth folly
Proverbs 15:18	A wrathful man stirreth up strife
Proverbs 19:19	A man of wrath shall suffer punishment
Proverbs 22:24	Make no friendship with an angry man
Colossians 3:21	Fathers, provoke not your children to anger

Notes

_____

_____

ANXIETY, WORRY, AND TENSION

Stress, which you experience as anxiety, worry, and tension, is one of the most destructive forces you can face. Stress is a product of our natural sinful state of being (self-consciousness). When under stress, you are concerned or troubled with distressing thoughts of real or imagined problems.

Stress occurs when you rely upon your own strength rather than upon God and His Word. It results from leaning upon your own understanding in dealing with problems. When you are anxious, you allow your carnal nature to persuade you that God is unable to handle the situation. Yet the Bible instructs you to cast all your anxieties on Him for He cares about you (1 Peter 5:7).

What Scripture Says

"No man can serve two masters: for either he will hate the one, and love the other; or else he will hold to the one, and despise the other. Ye cannot serve God and mammon. Therefore I say unto you, Take no thought for your life, what ye shall eat, or what ye shall drink, nor yet for your body, what ye shall put on. Is not the life more than meat, and the body than raiment? Behold the fowls of the air: for they sow not, neither do they reap, nor gather into barns; yet your heavenly Father feedeth them. Are ye not much better than they? Which of you by taking thought can add one cubit unto his stature? And why take ye thought for raiment? Consider the lilies of the field, how they grow; they toil not, neither do they spin: And yet I say unto you, That even Solomon in all his glory was not arrayed like one of these. Wherefore, if God so clothe the grass of the field, which today is, and tomorrow is cast into the oven, shall he not much more clothe you, O ye of little faith? Therefore take no thought, saying, What shall we eat? or, What shall we drink? or, Wherewithal shall we be clothed? (For after all these things do the Gentiles seek;) for your heavenly Father knoweth that ye have need of all these things. But seek ye first the kingdom of God and his righteousness; and all these things shall be added unto you. Take therefore no thought for the morrow; for the morrow shall take thought for the things of itself. Sufficient unto the day is the evil thereof" (Matthew 6:24-34).

"Trust in the Lord with all thine heart; and lean not unto thine own understanding. In all thy ways acknowledge him, and he shall direct thy paths" (Proverbs 3:5, 6).

"Be careful for nothing; but in every thing by prayer and supplication with thanksgiving let your requests be made known unto God" (Philippians 4:6).

"So that we may boldly say, The Lord is my helper, and I will not fear what man shall do unto me" (Hebrews 13:6).

How to Be Free

God wants you to be free from worry. Anxiety chokes the Word of God and keeps you from maturing in the Lord (Luke 8:14). Your faith and the corresponding strength to face problems are built up by the Word of God (Romans 10:17). If this strength and this growing process are cut off because of worry, you become an open target for Satan (1 Peter 5:8).

Don't give in to worry. Excuse yourself from "pity parties." Christ said in Matthew 6:33 to seek first His kingdom and His righteousness, and all these things shall be yours as well. Worry and frustration over the cares of this life won't change things. Your heavenly Father, however, knows your every need and will supply according to His promise.

Replace your worry and tension with prayer and thanksgiving (Philippians 4:6). Jesus is here right now to take your cares. He is your source of strength (Philippians 4:13). Take Him at His Word. Walk in His favor. Affirm daily that "I can do all things through Christ which strengtheneth me."

Learn and practice the principle of praise. As you praise God, He will honor your praise and minister to you in your need.

ANXIETY, WORRY, AND TENSION

As You Pray

Thank God that you can cast all your cares upon Him. Place all your problems on Him right now. Pray for the complete peace of God to be upon you.

Praise Him for meeting your needs. Agree in prayer with God and another believer that your needs are met, for God has promised that where two or more agree as touching any thing it shall be done (Matthew 18:19).

References/Homework

Matthew 13:22	Word of God choked
Luke 21:34	Don't let the cares of life cheat you out of salvation
Psalm 127:2	It is vain to be overly concerned about worldly cares
James 1:2	Count it joy when you meet trials
1 Corinthians 10:13	God has a way of escape; God is faithful
Matthew 25:14-27	Effects of worry
Hebrews 13:15	Sacrifice of praise to God
1 Thessalonians 5:18	Thank God in all things
Romans 8:28	All things work for your good
Psalm 22:3	Enthrone God, not your worry
Proverbs 12:25	Anxiety weighs one down
1 Samuel 17:47	The battle is the Lord's
Psalm 34:4	The Lord will deliver; the Lord answers
Psalm 56:9	God is for us
Joshua 10:24, 25	Our enemy is under foot
1 Kings 8:56	The Lord is faithful
Luke 12:22-32	Do not be anxious; seek His Kingdom

Read *What to Do About Worry,* Jay Adams.

BACKSLIDING

Backsliding occurs when a born-again believer in Christ turns back to sin or becomes stubborn in his heart and refuses to submit to the will of God in his life. The outward actions are only symptoms of the real problem—the attitude of the heart—which must be dealt with in order to change the actions.

Backsliding is like carnality in that your own desires and devices are acted out as opposed to God's will (1 Corinthians 3:3; Proverbs 14:14).

What Scripture Says

"Nevertheless I have somewhat against thee, because thou hast left thy first love. Remember therefore from whence thou art fallen, and repent, and do the first works; or else I will come unto thee quickly, and will remove thy candlestick out of his place, except thou repent" (Revelation 2:4, 5).

"If we confess our sins, he is faithful and just to forgive us our sins, and to cleanse us from all unrighteousness" (1 John 1:9).

"Wherefore he is able also to save them to the uttermost that come unto God by him, seeing he ever liveth to make intercession for them" (Hebrews 7:25).

"And when he came to himself, he said, How many hired servants of my father's have bread enough and to spare, and I perish with hunger! I will arise and go to my father, and will say unto him, Father, I have sinned against heaven, and before thee" (Luke 15:17, 18).

". . . let him return unto the Lord . . . for he will abundantly pardon" (Isaiah 55:7).

"I will heal their backsliding, I will love them freely . . ." (Hosea 14:4).

Does God Condemn Backsliders?

God does not condemn us—our own wickedness and backslidings do that (Jeremiah 2:19). Nor did Jesus come to do so, but to give us life abundantly (John 10:10). Therefore, if you will confess your sins, God will forgive you (1 John 1:9). Accept His forgiveness and then forgive yourself.

Forgive those who have wronged you. Go to anyone you have wronged or resented and ask their forgiveness. Make restitution in whatever ways you can for any wrongs your backsliding has caused.

If not baptized with the Holy Spirit, ask for and receive it (Luke 11:13). Then grow in Jesus and the way of the Lord. The Holy Spirit gives a Christian the ability to overcome sin. He gives power to be a Christ-like person. He guides, comforts, teaches spiritual truth, and equips with the gifts and qualities of God (Acts 1:8; John 14:16; 1 Corinthians 12; Galatians 5:22, 23).

As You Pray

Thank God for His compassion and mercy. Thank Him for taking you back into His loving grace now that you are returning to Him and for restoring peace, joy, and happiness to you as you become His servant again.

References/Homework

2 Chronicles 30:9	Grace assured at repentance
Psalms 32:1; 145:14	Blessed and upheld in the Lord
Isaiah 43:18, 19; 44:22	Old things are gone, the new redeems
John 3:17	No condemnation in Jesus

Read these Scriptures daily and memorize them for assurance of victory.

Notes

_____

_____

_____

BAPTISM/WATER

According to the Bible, to be baptized in water means to be immersed in water after being born again. The order of your relationship and experience in the Lord is first to believe and then to be baptized (Mark 16:16).

What Scripture Says

"Go ye therefore, and teach all nations, baptizing them in the name of the Father, and of the Son, and of the Holy Ghost" (Matthew 28:19).

"And why now tarriest thou? arise and be baptized, and wash away thy sins, calling on the name of the Lord" (Acts 22:16).

"Know ye not, that so many of us as were baptized into Jesus Christ were baptized into his death" (Romans 6:3).

"Buried with him in baptism, wherein also ye are risen with him through the faith of the operation of God, who hath raised him from the dead" (Colossians 2:12).

"The like figure whereunto even baptism doth also now save us [not the putting away of the filth of the flesh, but the answer of a good conscience toward God] by the resurrection of Jesus Christ" (1 Peter 3:21).

What Is Baptism?

Baptism is for a person who has been born again. The New Testament words *baptisma* and *baptizo* were not interpreted from the Greek text, but transliterated into English forms: *baptism* and *baptize*. "To baptize" means to completely immerse.

Those baptized by John the Baptist were completely immersed, as were those who believed in Jesus. Scripture tells us that there was always a body of water available, such as the Jordan where Jesus was baptized and the body of water available at the baptism of the

Ethiopian (Acts 8:33). Those being baptized went into and came up out of the water.

Baptism symbolizes and is a testimony of your identification with Christ's death, burial, and resurrection (see Romans 6:14ff.). It takes place after you have believed, as with the believers at Pentecost (Acts 2:41) and in Samaria (Acts 8:12), and with the Ethiopian (Acts 8:38), Paul (Acts 9:18), Lydia of Thyatira (Acts 16:15), the Philippian jailer (Acts 16:33), and the believers in Corinth (Acts 18:8) and Ephesus (Acts 19:5).

Baptism portrays your sins being forgiven and cleansed. Your sins are forgiven when you confess them (1 John 1:9). And you are cleansed by Jesus' shed blood (1 John 1:7). You are baptized to testify to that cleansing and forgiveness, not in order to be cleansed or forgiven.

Jesus had no sin. He was baptized to "fulfill righteousness." He identified Himself with John the Baptist's message. John baptized those who repented. It follows therefore, that a sin-free person is a candidate for baptism. Jesus was sin-free, and His baptism pleased the Father, who spoke on that occasion (Matthew 3:17).

New believers are to be baptized by baptized believers. Therefore, if you haven't been baptized, go to a body of baptized believers, share your testimony, and ask to be baptized according to the Bible.

As You Pray

Offer thanksgiving and praise for what God is doing in your life. Rejoice for God's great love toward you. Also pray and thank Him for other ways He wants to help you as you become more identified with Him.

References/Homework

Study Scriptures cited above and other references about baptism which you can find in a Bible concordance, such as Colossians 2:11, 12, and Ephesians 2:11-13.

Speak to a pastor at the church of your choice about being baptized and worshiping with the church fellowship.

BITTERNESS AND RESENTMENT

When you are offended or disappointed by others and allow the hurt to germinate in your heart, bitterness and resentment will take root. Characterized by an unforgiving spirit and generally negative, critical attitudes, bitterness and resentment are sinful and self-defeating. They will color your conscious and unconscious thoughts and actions. Allowed to fester, they will destroy and kill (Galatians 5:19-21). However, they can be dispelled with love.

What Scripture Says

"Follow peace with all men, and holiness, without which no man shall see the Lord: Looking diligently lest any man fail of the grace of God; lest any root of bitterness springing up trouble you, and thereby many be defiled" (Hebrews 12:14, 15).

"Let all bitterness, and wrath, and anger, and clamour, and evil speaking, be put away from you, with all malice: And be ye kind one to another, tenderhearted, forgiving one another, even as God for Christ's sake hath forgiven you" (Ephesians 4:31, 32).

"Who, when he was reviled, reviled not again, when he suffered, he threatened not; but committed himself to him that judgeth righteously" (1 Peter 2:23).

"Then said Jesus, Father, forgive them; for they know not what they do" (Luke 23:34).

"For if ye forgive men their trespasses, your heavenly Father will also forgive you: But if ye forgive not men their trespasses, neither will your Father forgive your trespasses" (Matthew 6:14, 15).

"Bless them which persecute you: bless, and curse not. Rejoice with them that do rejoice, and weep with them that weep. Be of the same mind one toward another. Mind not high things, but condescend to men of low estate. Be not wise in your own conceits. Recompense to no man evil for evil. Provide things honest in the sight of all men. If it be possible, as much as lieth in you, live peaceably with all men. Dearly beloved, avenge not yourselves, but rather give place unto wrath: for it is written, Vengeance is mine; I will repay, saith the Lord. Therefore if thine enemy hunger, feed him; if he thirst, give him drink: for in so doing thou shalt heap coals of fire on his head. Be not overcome of evil, but overcome evil with good" (Romans 12:14-21).

How to Be Free from Bitterness and Resentment

Like depression and other emotional stress, bitterness and resentment can aggravate or cause physical problems such as arthritis. You can be affected mentally, spiritually, and otherwise. Your relationships will always suffer.

God can free you from this sin. It is an oppressive and destructive emotion having its root in hate, which is likened to murder. You must repent. No one can have peace and happiness with such emotions tearing at him. If you have not done so, ask God to forgive you and to come into your life right now. He will deliver you from the power of the enemy (Psalm 91:3).

If you are already a Christian, you should still ask God to forgive you for being bitter and resentful. Then ask Him to forgive anyone who may have hurt you, and toward whom you are bitter or resentful, even as He forgives you.

Seek to be baptized with the Holy Spirit if you are not already. Look for opportunities to demonstrate love to the person who offended you.

God forgives and forgets sin. However, you may have made your best effort to forgive and forget and find that you cannot. God can help you to cleanse your memory. Instead of remembering with malice and hurt, remember with forgiveness. Then go one step further and ask God to forgive your offender. By forgiving and then asking God to forgive your offender, you release God to bless you and the other person.

BITTERNESS AND RESENTMENT

As You Pray

Pray in this manner:

Father, I acknowledge that I've held resentment and bitterness against _____. I confess this as sin and ask you to forgive me. I forgive _____. Remind me, Lord, to not hold any more resentments, but rather to love this person. Father, I ask you to also forgive _____. Thank you for hearing and answering my prayer. In Jesus' name, Amen.

References/Homework

Bitterness
Acts 8:23
Romans 3:14
Ephesians 4:31
Hebrews 12:15
James 3:14

Hatred
Leviticus 19:17
Proverbs 10:12
Proverbs 15:17
1 John 2:9
1 John 4:20

Envy
Psalm 37:1
Proverbs 3:31
Proverbs 23:17
Galatians 5:26
Genesis 26:14
Matthew 27:18

Malice
1 Corinthians 5:8; 14:20
Colossians 3:8
1 Peter 2:1
Esther 3:6
Psalm 140:3
Isaiah 59:4, 5
Matthew 27:23
John 12:10
Acts 7:54

Notes

_____

_____

_____

_____

_____

CHILD ABUSE

Child abuse may be a result of demon activity, compulsive behavior, drug and alcohol abuse, or similar problems. Frequently, a child becomes the innocent whipping post on which a parent or other caretaker vents his or her frustrations.

If you have a problem with child abuse, almost anything—even a small irritation—may provoke you to hurt your child. Or you may find that you strike out in uncontrollable rage when you are angry with the child or someone else such as your spouse or other children. Child abuse can also be emotional, sexual, or by neglect. The abuse of children is a serious matter in God's eyes as He says in Matthew 18:6: "But whoso shall offend one of these little ones which believe in me, it were better for him that a millstone were hanged about his neck, and that he were drowned in the depth of the sea." If you have this problem, God can help you.

It is necessary to keep ourselves under control, to strive for the mastery of all things. By doing so, we will obtain an incorruptible crown (1 Corinthians 9:25-27). Self-control (temperance) is obtained through the Holy Spirit (Galatians 5:22, 23).

What Scripture Says

"And every man that striveth for the mastery is temperate [has willpower] in all things. Now they do it to obtain a corruptible crown; but we an incorruptible. I therefore so run, not as uncertainly; so fight I, not as one that beateth the air: But I keep under my body, and bring it unto subjection: lest that by any means, when I have preached to others, I myself should be a castaway" (1 Corinthians 9:25-27).

"Among whom also we all had our conversation in times past in the lusts of our flesh, fulfilling the desires of the flesh and of the mind; and were by nature the children of wrath, even as others" (Ephesians 2:3).

"And, ye fathers, provoke not your children to wrath; but bring them up in the nurture and admonition of the Lord " (Ephesians 6:4).

"But put ye on the Lord Jesus Christ, and make not provision for the flesh, to fulfill the lusts thereof" (Romans 13:14).

"But the fruit of the Spirit is love, joy, peace, longsuffering, gentleness, goodness, faith, meekness, temperance: against such there is no law" (Galatians 5:22, 23).

What to Do about Child Abuse

Your first need is for salvation (Romans 6:23) and the baptism with the Holy Spirit. If you really want to change, you need the ability to do so. The Holy Spirit will give you that ability (Acts 1:8).

You also need the transformation that comes from renewing your mind. Start by repenting and asking Jesus to remove the rage you feel. Fellowship with Spirit-filled Christians can also help you overcome your problem.

Practice God's principle of praise. Focus your attention on God. Praise Him, the Problem Solver, instead of fighting the problem. He will help you. As a Christian empowered by the Holy Spirit, you will be able to overcome any compulsive temptation. You will be able to take authority over your anger in the name of Jesus. Don't let anger drive you. As you chase away these satanic, fleshly emotions, you will overcome your shortcomings and abilities rather than having them overcome you.

Seek help to bind any demonic spirits which cause a reprobate mind. A Spirit-filled Christian can command them to leave in Jesus' name. God wants you to be free even more than you do. He has someone available to help.

As You Pray

Pray for the Holy Spirit to anoint you, head to foot, and to completely cleanse your mind as you ask for forgiveness for your sin. Ask Christ to come into your life and fill you with the Holy Spirit and power.

Offer praise and thanksgiving for victory. God honors those who honor Him. Praise honor Him. Praise Him in all things. Speak His praises. Sing His praises. Persevere in praise until victory comes.

References/Homework

Philippians 4:4-9, 13	Instruction for growth in Jesus
Hebrews 1:14	Angels will minister for you
Romans 12:2	Renew your mind
James 4:7	Resist Satan
Romans 6	God's grace versus sinful behavior

Notes

_____

_____

_____

_____

_____

_____

_____

_____

CHURCH MEMBERSHIP

Is church membership necessary? What is a church? Which church is the one you should attend? God has answered these questions in His Word.

The Church is the body of Christ on earth and does the work of God. Christians are directed to assemble with the rest of the body of Christ (Hebrews 10:24, 25). Those who believe in Jesus and are born again have become God's children (2 Corinthians 6:18), and are heirs to the Kingdom along with Jesus (Romans 8:17). As God's children, Christians have certain rights, but they also have responsibilities as God's intercessors (Revelation 1:6).

What Scripture Says

"Then they that gladly received his word were baptized: and the same day there were added unto them [the Church] about three thousand souls" (Acts 2:41).

"And he is the head of the body, the church: who is the beginning, the firstborn from the dead; that in all things he might have the preeminence" (Colossians 1:18).

"For both he that sanctifieth and they [the Church] who are sanctified are all of one: for which cause he is not ashamed to call them brethren" (Hebrews 2:11).

"In this the children of God [the Church] are manifest, and the children of the devil: whosoever doeth not righteousness is not of God, neither he that loveth not his brother [the Church]" (1 John 3:10).

"Likewise greet the church that is in their house. Salute my well beloved Epaenetus, who is the firstfruits of Achaia unto Christ" (Romans 16:5).

The Church: Christ's Body

If we love Jesus, we must also love His Church. Every born-again Christian is a member of the greater body, referred to as the Church universal.

It is not a question of whether church membership is necessary. It is. But you need to determine of which local congregation you should be a part. Don't confuse the Church with a building. The Bible states that where two or three are gathered in the name of Jesus, He is in their midst. Therefore, a local congregation or church may consist of a group of two or three Christians meeting in someone's house.

Each local congregation is a member of the greater body of Christ. That means you should not turn your back on congregations other than your own. To do so would be to accuse them before God as not being His. And that is not for any man to judge. To love Christ is to love His Church—no matter what name or particular doctrine distinguishes one congregation from another.

Great wisdom is to be found among many counselors who are seeking God. Therefore, it is not good to be isolated from the rest of the body of Christ. Just as the gifts are given to individuals for the benefit of all, wisdom should be shared among many for the benefit of all (1 Corinthians 12:7).

How to Find a Local Church

The most important part of your relationship to Christ and His Church is that you are born again. After that, you need to be baptized in water and with the Holy Spirit. The Holy Spirit can then lead you to the right local church.

Which local church you should be part of is between you and God. You must determine where He wants you—both for your benefit and for the benefit of others in the body.

It is important to belong to a local church. When you commit yourself to be a part of the ministry of that church, you will experience greater spiritual growth. Then you will best be able to contribute your spiritual gifts and help meet the needs of the body of Christ for the edification of all.

As You Pray

As you seek God's will as to which local body you should join, thank and praise God for leading you to a Spirit-filled pastor and a Spirit-filled church. Expect Him to do so.

References/Homework

Revelation 1, 3	Strengths and weaknesses of churches
1 Corinthians 12	Each member has a function in the body
John 15	Necessary to abide in Jesus
1 Corinthians 13	Love is the key

Notes

_____

_____

_____

_____

_____

_____

_____

_____

_____

_____

COMPULSIVENESS

Compulsiveness can be described as a seemingly irresistible impulse or urge to act irrationally. Examples of compulsiveness may include: compulsive gambling, sex offenses, eating, talking, drinking, working, and child or spouse abuse.

If you suffer from compulsive behavior, you have a basic inability to be self-disciplined. You may also have a tendency to willfully yield to the lusts of the flesh listed in Galatians 5:19-21. Lasciviousness (lustful behavior) and revelings are closely allied to compulsiveness. As a result of yielding to the works of the flesh, you can come under demonic influence and you may be given over to a reprobate mind (Romans 1:28-32). But, God has a solution to your problem.

What Scripture Says

"And every man that striveth for the mastery is temperate in all things. Now they do it to obtain a corruptible crown; but we an incorruptible. I therefore so run, not as uncertainly; so fight I, not as one that beateth the air: But I keep under my body, and bring it into subjection: lest that by any means, when I have preached to others, I myself should be a castaway" (1 Corinthians 9:25-27).

"Among whom also we all had our conversation in times past in the lusts of our flesh, fulfilling the desires of the flesh and of the mind; and were by nature the children of wrath, even as others" (Ephesians 2:3).

"But put ye on the Lord Jesus Christ, and make not provision for the flesh, to fulfill the lusts thereof" (Romans 13:14).

"But the fruit of the Spirit is love, joy, peace, long suffering, gentleness, goodness, faith, meekness, temperance [self-control]: against such there is no law" (Galatians 5:22, 23).

COMPULSIVENESS

How to Overcome

To overcome compulsiveness, first assure yourself that you have been born again. Establish a firm, well-grounded relationship with Jesus Christ (Romans 3:23; 6:23).

Determine that Jesus will be Lord of your life. Consciously submit to the rulership of Jesus in your life. Then as a born-again Christian, deal with your flesh. Your basic nature is to be extremely self-conscious of your own person. The Bible describes our flesh and eyes as being lustful and our lives (personage) as being proud (1 John 2:16). A product of our natural sin of self-consciousness is the sin of compulsiveness. The fleshly lusts take control.

The secret to defeating the works of the flesh is not only exercising more willpower or trying harder, but also reckoning your flesh dead and buried with Christ. If a Christian, you now live in the newness of Jesus' resurrection life and power. Read Romans 6:1-13. The key idea in this passage is "to reckon" in verse 11. This refers to an active, conscious, mental process whereby you affirm the truth of God's Word in your situation.

Your best offense against compulsiveness is to focus your attention on God, the Problem Solver, rather than continually focusing on the problem. Turn your problem into a blessing. The Bible says to thank God for all things and in all things (Ephesians 5:20; 1 Thessalonians 5:18). God works it for your good if you put your love and trust in Him (Romans 8:28).

Daily, and especially at every temptation to do a compulsive act, whether out of anger, frustration, nervous tension, fleshly desire, or force of habit, follow a simple pattern which will begin to transform and renew your mind (Romans 12:2). First of all, thank God for the problem, the temptation or the habit. Thank and praise Him for revealing it to you, and for providing a way out of it. There is always a way of escape (1 Corinthians 10:13). He will show you what, where and how.

Next, begin to put your mind on Christ rather than on the problem. You need peace and freedom in the face of it. Offer praise (honor and respect) and thanksgiving to God until peace and joy come (Isaiah

26:3). Make a sacrifice of continual praise. Persevere, knowing that God will honor your praise and minister to you.

As You Pray

As soon as you recognize a compulsive desire, pray and renounce it. Then pray for God to deliver you from the desire. Pray to receive the fruit of the Spirit, especially temperance (willpower). Pray in agreement with a prayer partner that God "is overcoming compulsiveness within you."

References/Homework

Philippians 4:4-13	Growth in Christ
Galatians 5:19-21	Works of the flesh listed
Galatians 5:22, 23	Fruit of the Spirit listed

Notes

_____

_____

_____

_____

_____

_____

_____

_____

_____

COVETOUSNESS

The sin of covetousness is a continuing and abiding desire to have that which you do not now possess, control, or otherwise have access to, use of, or authority over. The Bible says:

"Thou shalt not covet thy neighbour's house, thou shalt not covet thy neighbour's wife, nor his manservant, nor his maidservant, nor his ox, nor his ass, nor any thing that is thy neighbour's" (Exodus 20:17).

But it is a good thing to covet God's gifts:

"But covet earnestly the best gifts: and yet shew I unto you a more excellent way [love]" (1 Corinthians 12:31).

How to Overcome the Sin of Covetousness

As a born-again Christian, you can overcome the sin of covetousness. Confess and repent of being covetous. Ask God to forgive and cleanse you (1 John 1:9). Ask God to fill you with His Holy Spirit to give you the power to overcome (Luke 11:13).

Scripture says you can put off covetousness by inclining your heart toward God (Psalm 119:36). As you submit yourself to God, you will be strengthened to resist and break any fleshly desire to covet.

As you seek God and the things of God (Colossians 3:1-4), you will discover that your desire to have what belongs to another is replaced with an inner contentment. Begin meditating on God's Word so that you may be transformed into the image of Christ. Then you will be able to bless others, rather than covet their possessions. You are what you think. Therefore, it is important to fill your mind with godly thoughts. One way to do this is by reading God's Word and books which testify of God's working in people's lives.

Gifts to Be Coveted

To covet (seek after) the good gifts of God, ask for them. Be especially sure to ask for a spiritual gift when you need it. Study carefully the Scriptures concerning the gifts of the Spirit (1 Peter 4; Romans 12; Ephesians 4; 1 Corinthians 12). As a Spirit-filled Christian, you are to do the work of God. The gifts of the Spirit are to equip you, to confirm God's Word and to bless others.

As you grow in God's Word and in faith, the coveted gifts (and others not coveted) will be quickened in you. Fellowshipping with Christians who are experiencing the results of the ministry of the gifts will help you learn more about the gifts. Expect faith to rise up in you as you offer quiet praise to God.

As You Pray

Confess and repent of the sin of covetousness.

Praise and thank God for transforming your desires. Praise and thank Him for His gifts to the church and to you as you need them in order to bless and minister to other people.

References/Homework

Hebrews 13:15   Praise God continually
1 John 1:9   Commit covetousness to God

Notes

_____

_____

_____

_____

_____

_____

_____

_____

CULTS

To the Christian, a cult can be defined as any group that has a form of godliness, but does not recognize Jesus Christ as the unique Son of God. Walter R. Martin in *The Kingdom of the Cults* states that a cult "is a religious group which differs significantly in one or more respects as to belief or practice, from those religious groups which are regarded as the normative expressions of religion in our total culture." It may be oriented around a personality or around a "revelation" or "interpretation" of one individual. For example, Jehovah's Witnesses are, for the most part, followers of the interpretations and teachings of Charles T. Russell and J. F. Rutherford. Mormons are followers of the interpretations and teachings of Joseph Smith and Brigham Young.

There are many kinds of religions in the world today. Each group says that theirs is a true religion. However, if you wish to know the true and living God, you must receive the Word of God with all readiness of mind and search the Scriptures daily, to find "whether those things are so" (Acts 17:11b).

What Scripture Says

"Through thy precepts I get understanding: therefore I hate every false way" (Psalm 119:104).

"And then if any man shall say to you, Lo, here is Christ; or lo, he is there; believe him not: For false Christs and false prophets shall rise, and shall shew signs and wonders, to seduce, if it were possible, even the elect. But take ye heed: behold, I have foretold you all things" (Mark 13:21-23).

"For such are false apostles, deceitful workers, transforming themselves into the apostles of Christ. And no marvel; for Satan himself is transformed into an angel of light. Therefore it is no great thing if his ministers also be transformed as the ministers of righteousness;

whose end shall be according to their works" (2 Corinthians 11:13-15).

How to Recognize a Cult

When you know the truth, that which is authentic, you will easily recognize the "less than authentic." Take the Bible at face value in all its simplicity. Search the Bible, to judge whether a teaching is cultish. See if it deviates from God's Word so as to pervert the clear teaching on important matters of faith and practice. These matters include: the doctrine of God (Father, Son and Holy Spirit); heaven; hell; Satan; salvation; baptism; baptism with the Holy Spirit; matters of righteousness and holiness in the Lord; the Second Coming of Christ; the resurrection of the dead and recognition of the Bible as the guide and truth for faith and practice.

One test of a cult is that it often does not strictly teach that Jesus is the only begotten Son of God who Himself is God manifested in the flesh. Another test is whether the person who is the teacher or leader of the group or movement promotes himself as being equal to or greater than Jesus, or promotes allegiance to himself in such a way as to take away from obedience to and worship of Christ (2 Corinthians 10:10, 18; 11:3, 4).

Christian-oriented cults include: The Church of the Latter-day Saints or Reorganized Church of Latter-day Saints (also known as Mormons); the Worldwide Church of God (Armstrongism); Christian Science; Unity; Unitarianism (various groups); The Way International (not all groups using the term "The Way"); Rosicrucian Society of America; Bahai; Hare Krishna; Scientology; The Unification Church ("Moonies"); the so-called "Children of God" headed by "Moses" Berg; Jehovah's Witnesses and other fringe groups whose teachings should be suspect.

Some occult groups mix Christianity into their teachings, often deceiving people into following them. Included are: The Association for Research and Enlightenment (ARE); Theosophy; witchcraft and others. Also beware of groups following "Cabalism"; lodges having secret and often bloody oaths; Transcendental Meditation (TM); eastern mysticism (including yoga and those where deities are named) and others which would add Christianity to their religious practices and beliefs.

If you have been entangled with any of these groups, repent, renouncing your involvement with them. Call on the Lord Jesus for forgiveness and cleansing (1 John 1:9) and ask for the baptism with the Holy Spirit (Acts 1:8). Participate in a local church fellowship and church-recognized Holy Spirit-oriented Bible/prayer fellowship where the Bible is the only rule for faith and practice (Acts 17:11b).

Upon renouncing cultish beliefs and activities, you must still make willful choices that will change habit patterns related to the cultish activity. Old patterns (e.g., inordinate cult-oriented meditation) carried over into a new Christian lifestyle (e.g., prayer) tends to deceive and weaken your resistance to future satanic attacks, much as hypnotism weakens your ability to resist repeated hypnosis.

As you Pray

Repent of cultish involvement. If you find that you cannot repent, you need to seek help for deliverance from cultish spirits. Pray for spiritual enlightenment. Pray that the Holy Spirit will lead you to a church fellowship that teaches Bible truth.

References/Homework

Read *The Kingdom of the Cults,* Walter Martin.

Galatians 1:8, 9	Warning on non-gospel teaching
2 Corinthians 11:13-15	False apostles
Mark 13:21-23	False messiahs
2 Timothy 4:1-5	Admonition toward correct teaching
Deuteronomy 13:1-5; 18:20, 22	Warning about false prophets and dreamers
Jeremiah 23	Destructiveness of unfaithful pastors

DELIVERANCE

You need deliverance when you are unable to free yourself from a bondage, whether mental (emotional), physical or spiritual. It may be associated with demonic activity or a yielding to selfish desires. The problem could reveal itself in the form of compulsive impulses, over-indulgence, perverted behavior, or other unacceptable life-styles. You may have a general or specific inability to even repent of sin and receive Christ in salvation or to repent of backsliding.

What Scripture Says

"When the even was come, they brought unto him many that were possessed with devils: and he cast out the spirits with his word, and healed all that were sick" (Matthew 8:16).

"And Jesus rebuked the devil; and he departed out of him: and the child was cured from that very hour" (Matthew 17:18).

"He that believeth and is baptized shall be saved; but he that believeth not shall be damned. And these signs shall follow them that believe; In my name shall they cast out devils; they shall speak with new tongues; They shall take up serpents; and if they drink any deadly thing, it shall not hurt them; they shall lay hands on the sick, and they shall recover" (Mark 16:16-18).

"Watch and pray, that ye enter not into temptation: the spirit indeed is willing, but the flesh is weak" (Matthew 26:41).

"For we know that the law is spiritual: but I am carnal, sold under sin" (Romans 7:14).

You must recognize your need and discern what your problem is. Our warfare is with the forces of evil (Ephesians 6:12). Our armor is truth, righteousness, preparation to witness to the gospel, faith and salvation. Our weapon is the Word of God. The battle is one involving prayer (Ephesians 6:14-18). Our authority and power are from Jesus Himself (Mark 16:17; Acts 1:8). The battlefield is first of all in spiritual realms. Ask someone such as your pastor or another Spirit-filled person to agree with you in prayer and stand with you against any demonic influence. Ask him to seek the Lord in your behalf for discernment concerning your need. We often enter into bondage because of yielding to fleshly desires (Galatians 5:19-21). If your bondage is discerned as demonic, ask your Spirit-filled prayer partner to take authority in the name of Jesus, claiming God's protection for you and others in the vicinity. Ask him to bind the demons, revealed and unrevealed. As he commands them to loose you and come out of you, in Jesus' name, they must go where God sends them.

With your prayer partner, at home and at church, you should spend time in praise to God, giving Him preeminence in the matter. Call on God to send angels to help (Hebrews 1:14).

Seek fellowship with Spirit-filled people. Bible study is important (2 Timothy 2:15). A renewed mind will transform you (Romans 12:2). Attend a Spirit-filled church for further help and for aid in spiritual growth (Hebrews 10:25).

To stay free, you need to receive both forgiveness of sin and the baptism with the Holy Spirit. Ask the Lord to baptize you. He will keep His promise as you ask (Luke 11:13). For help in understanding and for prayer in helping you to receive the Holy Spirit, ask another Spirit-filled Christian to agree with you in prayer.

How to Pray

If you are in bondage to sin, confess and repent of any sin in your life which has you bound, asking God to forgive you. You will never be set free until you confront and deal with your sin at the cross (Romans 6:23; 1 John 1:8, 9; John 8:36).

If demonic bondage is discerned, pray in agreement with another person who is a Christian. Satan and his demons should be bound in Jesus' name (Luke 10:17).

Be firm and bold in your determination to be free (1 John 4:4).

Minister praise to God until the victory comes, the burden is lifted, and Satan has fled (Psalm 150:1-6).

DELIVERANCE

References/Homework

Read *Defeated Enemies,* Corrie Ten Boom; *Demons in the World Today,* Merrill Unger.

Examples of Deliverance
1 Samuel 17:37—David
Daniel 6:22—Daniel
Acts 5:18, 19; 12:7; 16:26
—Apostles

Overcoming in the Spirit
1 Thessalonians 5:16-23
Romans 8:9
Galatians 5:22, 23
1 Corinthians 14:4, 15

Deliverance Promised
James 5:15—From Disease
2 Timothy 4:18—From Evil
  Works
2 Peter 2:9—From Temptation

Authority to Deliver
Mark 16:17
John 14:12

1 Corinthians 12:8-11

Deliverance Received
Mark 5:1-15

Notes

_____

_____

_____

_____

_____

_____

_____

_____

DEPRESSION/ DISCOURAGEMENT

If you are depressed, you are suffering from one of the most common emotional problems people experience. When you are depressed, you feel sad, discouraged, and unable to get "on top of things."

The basic cause of depression is sin (Psalm 38:3-8). Out of a sense of hopelessness, failure or inadequacy (even caused by small things), you may begin to dislike yourself (Job 3). This may result in a distrust of God, resentment of others and self-pity—all of which lead to more feelings of guilt and depression and more inactivity, doubting, complaining and worrying. Eventually, you may feel trapped in an inescapable pit (James 1:14, 15).

What Scripture Says
"For the thing which I greatly feared is come upon me, and that which I was afraid of is come unto me" (Job 3:25).

"For I acknowledge my transgressions: and my sin is ever before me. . . . Restore unto me the joy of thy salvation; and uphold me with thy free spirit" (Psalm 51:3, 12).

"And we know that all things work together for good to them that love God, to them who are the called according to his purpose" (Romans 8:28).

"In everything give thanks: for this is the will of God in Christ Jesus concerning you" (1 Thessalonians 5:18).

"And when ye stand praying, forgive, if ye have aught against any: that your Father also which is in heaven may forgive you your trespasses" (Mark 11:25).

"Come unto me, all ye that labour and are heavy laden, and I will give you rest. Take my yoke upon you, and learn of me; for I am meek and lowly in heart: and ye shall find rest unto your souls. For my yoke is easy, and my burden is light" (Matthew 11:28-30).

DEPRESSION/DISCOURAGEMENT

How to Recognize Depression and Discouragement

The symptoms of depression include: physical—trouble sleeping, loss of appetite, loss of weight, loss of interest in sex, complaints about the body, lack of energy; thinking patterns—problems with concentration, poor memory, trouble making decisions, excessive self-criticism, thoughts of death or suicide; emotions—hopelessness, guilt, irritability, crying, fear, gloomy outlook (sometimes covered up by opposite behavior such as giddy, inappropriate laughing, or being very quiet and sweet); activity—slowing of most activity, withdrawal from social contacts, deterioration of work and personal appearance. If you are depressed, you may display irresponsible behavior and attitudes and be increasingly dependent on feelings. Loss of control and an accompanying mental and emotional breakdown may follow.

Recognize and take seriously the depth of your depression. It may not be enough to tell yourself: "I must cheer up and snap out of it," or "I shouldn't feel this way because things can't be so bad."

Talk to your pastor or other Christian counselor. Tell him that this problem is really bothering you. He is there to help you. Together, the two of you can begin to find out how the depression began and what to do about it. Pray together and ask the Holy Spirit to reveal the roots of the depression. Some causes are:

Relationships with others—husband/wife, children, church, parents, relatives, neighbors, and fellow employees;

Physical problems—medications, drugs, alcohol or lack of sleep or exercise may cause or indicate depression or discouragement; and in women, childbirth, menstruation or menopause may be factors;

Disorganization—laziness, avoidance of a difficult task, poor work habits, unresolved pressures at work, unfinished jobs;

Self-condemnation—from obvious sin and resulting guilt, such as dishonesty, sexual lapses, failure to witness, failure to fulfill responsibility;

Financial and material problems—resulting from gambling, installment buying, etc.;

Loneliness, fear, self-pity, self-condemnation;

Demonic activity where any of the above may indicate such.

DEPRESSION/DISCOURAGEMENT

How to Overcome Depression and Discouragement

If you have been experiencing defeat in life, you need to begin living according to biblical principles. Begin by making sure you have been born again by the Spirit of God. If you are not certain, ask God right now to forgive you for your sins and to come into your life (Romans 10:9, 10, 13; 1 John 1:8, 9; John 1:12).

Once you have experienced the new birth in Christ, you need the ability to live like you are Christ's. You need Jesus to baptize you with the Holy Spirit. Ask Him to do it (Luke 11:13).

The Holy Spirit guides, comforts, teaches, empowers and produces the very qualities of God within a Christian (John 16:7-15; Galatians 5:22, 23).

Deal with wrong patterns and habits you may have in the light of Scripture. With God's help, take specific action regarding what needs to be eliminated and what should replace it.

Anything less than faith in God and His Word is sin. Therefore, recognize depression as a result of sin. Repent of your lack of faith. God will forgive and cleanse you (1 John 1:9). Begin to renew your mind with positive actions. Deal with habits and behavior patterns in the light of Scripture.

Positive action includes confessing: "I can do all things through Christ which strengtheneth me . . . " (Philippians 4:13); "My God [is supplying] all my needs according to His riches in glory by Christ Jesus" (Philippians 4:19); "For God hath not given me a spirit of fear: but of power, and of love, and of a sound mind" (2 Timothy 1:7); "God is giving me power over all the power of the enemy: and nothing shall by any means hurt me" (Luke 10:19); "I am more than conqueror through Him that loves me" (Romans 8:37); "I am healed by the stripes of Jesus" (1 Peter 2:24; Isaiah 53:5).

Do not determine on your own that you are experiencing a demonic depression. Rather, seek help from your pastor or other qualified Christian counselor. If you do suspect demon activity, begin to glorify God in praise and thanksgiving. Satan does not like to stay where God is glorified. Repent of any known sin. Claim God's forgiveness and cleansing (1 John 1:9).

Let a Christian pastor or counselor help you. Rebuild your spiritual life through Bible reading, prayer, and fellowship with other Christians. Attend a local Bible-believing church faithfully. When you "sink your roots" in a church, you will begin experiencing overcoming faith and spiritual growth.

God can also heal any physical problem that causes, or is caused by, depression. If your doctor has diagnosed a particular problem, ask your prayer partner, pastor, Christian counselor or other Christian to agree with you in prayer for God's healing. If you are taking medication for the problem, your doctor should be able to determine whether it should be changed or stopped. A simple diet change may be your need. Consult your doctor and/or a dietician.

As You Pray

In prayer, thank God for His love and for revealing specific sins to you. Forgive others. Thank Him for healing you and renewing your joy.

References/Homework

Read *How to Win Over Depression,* Tim LaHaye.

Philippians 4:4-13   Growth in Christ
Begin doing unfinished work.

Notes

_____

_____

_____

_____

_____

_____

_____

_____

_____

DISCIPLINE/CHILD

It is the nature of most, if not all, children to be disobedient and/or rebellious toward parents, guardians and/or other authorities. It is normal and to be expected. Yet the Bible says rebellion is as the sin of witchcraft and must be corrected for the sake of the child and all concerned.

When a child is brought up according to scriptural principles, he will continue to follow those principles later in life. The Bible clearly teaches that parents or guardians are responsible for training and disciplining their children until the time that the children are no longer dependent upon them (Proverbs 22:6).

What Scripture Says

"And thou shalt love the Lord thy God with all thine heart, and with all thy soul, and with all thy might. And these words, which I command thee this day, shall be in thine heart: And *thou shalt teach them* diligently *unto thy children,* and shalt talk of them when thou sittest in thine house, and when thou walkest by the way, and when thou liest down, and when thou risest up" (Deuteronomy 6:5-7).

"Train up a child in the way he should go: and when he is old, he will not depart from it" (Proverbs 22:6).

"Chasten thy son while there is hope, and let not thy soul spare for his crying" (Proverbs 19:18).

"He that spareth his rod *hateth* his son: but *he that loveth him chasteneth* him betimes" (Proverbs 13:24).

"Foolishness is bound in the heart of a child; but the rod of correction shall drive it far from him" (Proverbs 22:15).

"And, ye fathers, provoke not your children to wrath: but bring them up in the nurture and admonition of the Lord" (Ephesians 6:4).

"One that ruleth well his own house, having his children in subjection with all gravity" (1 Timothy 3:4, qualifications for spiritual leaders).

"That they may teach the young women to be sober, to love their husbands, to love their children" (Titus 2:4).

Suggestions on Child Discipline

Your first concern should always be a child's salvation relationship with Christ. A child who has a good knowledge of the Bible gained through his church's Bible classes and your family's daily religious devotions will have a foundation for life that can't be equaled.

In communicating with your children, speak to them on their own level of understanding. Make it clear what you expect of them. Do not punish them in anger. Set the example you want them to follow, remembering that what you do will be more effective than what you say. When you establish guidelines for children, stick to them. Take your children with you to church and let them see you worship God and pray.

Father and mother, if both are in the family, *must* present a unified front. There should be no parental disagreement in front of a child. Make it clear that the mother's authority is derived from the father. Don't be wishy-washy. Be specific in all instructions and discipline.

Recognize and teach a child that parental responsibility extends over public school education, club, group, or any organization's efforts or influences. Parents or guardians must be faithful to teach a child about Christ. His promises are yea! and amen! concerning your child.

Ask the Lord to show you how to properly discipline your children. Determine if there is a situation in the home which is directly contributing to any behavior problems which may exist, such as the mother working, etc. Administer discipline according to the child's age and transgression. The rules of discipline should be:
- Never discipline in anger.
- Always explain why you are disciplining the child.
- Demonstrate your love afterwards.
- Always express forgiveness afterwards.
- Never mention the subject again—treat the child as if it never happened.

DISCIPLINE/CHILD

- Follow through with discipline. Make sure a command is obeyed.
- Punish disobedience.

If you make a mistake, apologize and ask forgiveness. And remember, nothing will substitute for spending time with a child. Ask God to give you a great love for your children. Note all the praiseworthy things about each child and share them with him. In this way, you will encourage him rather than discourage him. Ask God to show you ways to bless each child.

If you find yourself being constantly critical, it may be that you need to recognize the individuality of the child. You should not expect him to be a carbon copy of you. Each child has certain natural, God-given gifts and abilities. Look for these talents and encourage the child in these areas.

As You Pray

Pray with your children encouraging them to join in prayer with you and assure them that you will continue to pray for them. If necessary, lead them in a model prayer.

Spend time in prayer daily for your children. In biblical times, it was traditional with God's people, the Jews, to pronounce a blessing upon their children. You can do the same. Bless your children with a benediction of love and encouragement as you pray.

References/Homework

Read *Dare to Discipline* by James Dobson, and other books recommended by your pastor or religious bookstore.

Deuteronomy 4:9	Instruction
Proverbs 8:32; 10:1	Exhortation
Proverbs 13:24; 22:15	Correction
Ephesians 6:1-13	Exhortation
Luke 2:49; 2 Timothy 3:15	Exhortation

Notes

_____

_____

DISCIPLING

Every born-again believer needs help in maintaining victory and gaining maturity in his life as a Christian. You can help a new Christian grow spiritually in the Lord.

A Christian is endued with power when the Holy Spirit comes upon him (Acts 1:8). With the laying on of hands, he receives the Holy Spirit. But his gifts need stirring up and he needs to grow and mature. Every "Timothy" needs a "Paul" to disciple him (2 Timothy 1:6).

What Scripture Says

"He that loveth father or mother more than me is not worthy of me: and he that loveth son or daughter more than me is not worthy of me: and he that taketh not his cross, and followeth after me, is not worthy of me" (Matthew 10:37, 38).

". . . If ye continue in my word, then are ye my disciples indeed" (John 8:31).

". . . If any man will come after me, let him deny himself, and take up his cross daily, and follow me" (Luke 9:23).

"But ye shall receive power, after that the Holy Ghost is come upon you: and ye shall be witnesses unto me both in Jerusalem, and in all Judaea, and in Samaria, and unto the uttermost part of the earth" (Acts 1:8).

"Go ye therefore, and teach all nations, baptizing them in the name of the Father, and of the Son, and of the Holy Ghost" (Matthew 28:19).

How to Disciple Another

It is God's will for all His children to be Jesus' disciples. Yet discipleship, like salvation, is never forced. A disciple is someone who receives the teaching of another. The teacher must himself walk in the light of God's Word. Through the discipleship experience, both

DISCIPLING

teacher and disciple are taught by the Holy Spirit using God's Word. Both are being conformed to God's image, with the Teacher of both being the Holy Spirit.

In order to disciple another, you must first be a disciple. Here are some steps to becoming a disciple of the Lord Jesus:

First, totally surrender yourself to the lordship of Jesus. Resolve to do God's will as totally as Jesus did in Gethsemane. Determine in your heart, "not *my* will but Thine," in all matters, present and future. Remember, as you seek God's will, you must be willing to obey it.

Self must be "crucified" in your daily life to release God's resurrection power. As self decreases, Christ increases. When this takes place, it is no longer you, but Christ who lives in you and is seen by others in your life.

Consistency and time are keys to spiritual growth. Join a directed Bible study effort with other Christians. You may also wish to undertake a self-study program which may be obtained through your church, religious bookstore, or by correspondence through many other ministries. Join other mature Christians in a ministry of witnessing to other people, such as an outreach of your local church.

There are many good Scripture memory kits available. Set aside time daily to learn and memorize Scripture about salvation, soul-winning, and God's promises to those who believe.

Using a chain reference Bible, a concordance, a Bible dictionary, and/or a good teacher's topical reference Bible, study the great doctrines of the Church. These include: God, Christ, teachings about the Holy Spirit, heaven, hell, angels, sin, and the Church itself. Study the great biblical principles and concepts such as those in Pat Robertson's *The Secret Kingdom.* Take good notes that you can use in teaching another.

Six major areas of spiritual growth for a disciple of Christ are: salvation, the baptism with the Holy Spirit, putting on God's armor, receiving the fruit of the Holy Spirit, growing under the ministries of the Holy Spirit, and receiving the gifts of the Spirit for witnessing about Christ. You will mature to a fullness of the measure of Christ as you learn, receive and live in God's full counsel.

It is important to be careful not to demand that you be followed as "the teacher." Lift up Jesus. The Holy Spirit magnifies Christ. Do likewise. When He is lifted up, men are drawn to Him.

There is always a time when you have taught all you can teach. If you have been consistent in pointing a new disciple to Christ and seeing to it that he is finding his place within the fellowship of his church, you will have succeeded as a "discipler." The new disciple, having received from you, must be turned loose to disciple others.

As You Pray

Pray in intercession for the person(s) God places in your trust. Yielding to His will, seek to know what He would have you do daily and also with your life in general. Thank Him for leading you and for allowing you to be a blessing to others from this moment on.

References/Homework

Recommended reading: Andrew Murray's booklet, "School of Obedience," and *The Secret Kingdom* by Pat Robertson with Bob Slosser.

Using a concordance, make a study on "discipleship" and "obedience."

1 and 2 Timothy; Luke 11:13; Acts 2; John 3, 14, 16; Galatians 5:22, 23; Ephesians 4:11-13; 6:11-18; Romans 12; 1 Corinthians 12; Mark 16:9-20.

Notes

_____

_____

_____

_____

_____

_____

_____

_____

DIVORCE

Divorce, whether it is being contemplated or a fact, is never pleasant nor is it desired. God's Word never supports divorce, but does offer guidance, encouragement, hope and love to those involved.

Many factors can contribute to the dissolution of a marriage, but the central cause is generally selfishness. As each partner demands his own way, Satan will take advantage of the situation, which might cause greater division and the eventual dissolving of the relationship. However, we must recognize that no problems are solved by lowering God's standards for marriage established in His Word (James 1:25; 1 Peter 5:8).

What Scripture Says

". . . Is it lawful for a man to put away his wife for every cause? And he answered and said unto them, Have ye not read, that he which made them at the beginning made them male and female. And said, For this cause shall a man leave father and mother, and shall cleave to his wife: And they twain shall be one flesh? Wherefore they are no more twain, but one flesh. What therefore God hath joined together, let not man put asunder. They say unto him, Why did Moses then command to give a writing of divorcement, and to put her away? He saith unto them, Moses because of the hardness of your hearts suffered you to put away your wives: But from the beginning it was not so. And I say unto you, Whosoever shall put away his wife, except it be for fornication, and shall marry another, committeth adultery: And whoso marrieth her which is put away doth commit adultery" (Matthew 19:3b-9).

"And unto the married I command, yet not I, but the Lord, Let not the wife depart from her husband: But and if she depart, let her remain unmarried, or be reconciled to her husband: And let not the husband put away his wife. But to the rest speak I, not the Lord: If any brother hath a wife that believeth not, and she be pleased to dwell with him, let him not put her away. And the woman which hath an husband that believeth not, and if he be pleased to dwell with her, let her not leave him. For the unbelieving husband is sanctified by the wife, and the unbelieving wife is sanctified by the husband: else were your children unclean; but now are they holy. But if the unbelieving depart, let him depart. A brother or a sister is not under bondage in such cases: but God hath called us to peace" (1 Corinthians 7:10-15).

"When Jesus had lifted up himself, and saw none but the woman, he said unto her, Woman, where are those thine accusers? Hath no man condemned thee? She said, No man, Lord. And Jesus said unto her, Neither do I condemn thee: Go, and sin no more" (John 8:10, 11).

When Reconciliation Is Possible

If you are questioning whether divorce is honored by God, the answer, obviously, is no. God hates divorce. There is no concession for not loving one another. Surrender yourself, your spouse and your family to God right now. Trust Him to be faithful in His promises.

If neither of you have remarried, determine to make every effort to effect reconciliation. Trust God to do all in His power to help you. If you are a born-again Christian, be willing to take the initiative with one-sided steps toward reconciliation.

Your first need is to confess and repent of any sin in your life. Ask other Christians to agree with you in prayer for your spouse's salvation and growth in the Lord. Your motive should be: Salvation and growth for your sake and for your spouse's sake, rather than merely for your welfare, pride or personal vindication. If others are involved, such as a third party, pray for God's forgiveness of them. You must release them to Him for your own sake, and theirs (1 John 2:8-11).

Finally, you and your family are so important to God that He has someone ready to help. You don't have to try to work things out alone. Seek the help of a pastor or Christian counselor.

DIVORCE

When Reconciliation Is Not Possible

If your past lifestyle has failed, God has a better plan. Begin your new life by reorienting yourself (Romans 12:2). Seek counsel and spiritual help. Christian fellowship and knowledge of God's Word are indispensable in helping you to avoid previous mistakes. You need to grow spiritually and have the understanding and support of God's family, the Church. Accept no substitute. Avoid the mistake made by so many who seek an answer to loneliness, hurt, frustration, etc., in the wrong places.

Divorce is not the unpardonable sin. Even to those who had been caught in sin, Jesus forgave them with admonishment, "go your way and sin no more" (John 4:1-42; 8:10, 11).

Admit your error, confess your sin and repent. There must be repentance (1 John 1:8, 9; 2:9-11). Then go on with a renewed dedication to God. The temptation to hate your spouse or others involved must be resisted (1 John 2:8-11). In order that you not fall victim to bitterness, resentment and desire for revenge, God's Word says that you must be willing to forgive.

Even as you ask God to forgive your sinful attitudes, actions, etc., ask Him to also forgive your estranged spouse and any others involved (such as a third party.) It is then that you can ask God to give you a love for your spouse and any others. Praise Him for doing it. As you honor God with that praise, He will honor you (1 Samuel 2:30b). His desire is that you have your physical, emotional and spiritual health restored. As you bless those who despitefully use you, or treat you cruelly in any way, God will bless you. What you sow now is what you will also reap.

As You Pray

Ask God to forgive all those involved and to produce the fruit of the Spirit "love" in all concerned. Pray for the fruit of the Spirit love, joy, peace, etc., to be produced within you.

If you are a born-again Christian, you can rebuke Satan for trying to destroy you, your family and others involved. Stand against him and with your spouse. You can be the intercessor. Don't give Satan any concession. Be firm against him, in Jesus' name. Above all,

64

minister praise to God (the Overcomer). He will honor your praise. Trust in Him. He will give you peace in your time of need.

References/Homework

Read *Divorce*, John Murray; *The Christian Family*, Larry Christenson.

1 Corinthians 13	Love in action
Galatians 5	Flesh and Spirit
John 15	Sticking to Jesus
Hebrews 11	Faith
Ephesians 5	Duty to the spouses
Colossians 3	Duty to the spouses
1 Corinthians 7	The marriage bond
1 Peter 3:1-7	Responsibilities of spouses

Notes

_____

_____

_____

_____

_____

_____

_____

_____

_____

DRUGS

Are you enslaved or troubled by a habitual use of various narcotic, stimulant, or mind-influencing drugs (including alcohol)? Do you have symptoms of physical, emotional or mental addiction? You may not have a sickness, but a sin problem which causes enslavement and sickness.

Jesus Christ has done something about your problem. He came to liberate you from such problems and enable you to gain self-control, a fruit of the Holy Spirit (Galatians 5:22, 23).

What Scripture Says

"All things are lawful unto me, but all things are not expedient: all things are lawful for me, but I will not be brought under the power of any" (1 Corinthians 6:12).

"And be not drunk with wine [or high on other drugs], wherein is excess; but be filled with the Spirit" (Ephesians 5:18).

"The Spirit of the Lord is upon me, because he hath anointed me to preach the gospel to the poor; he hath sent me to heal the broken-hearted, to preach deliverance to the captives, and recovering of sight to the blind, to set at liberty them that are bruised. To preach the acceptable year of the Lord. And he closed the book, and he gave it again to the minister, and sat down. And the eyes of all them that were in the synagogue were fastened on him. And he began to say unto them, This day is this scripture fulfilled in your ears. . . . And they were all amazed, and spake among themselves, saying, What a word is this! For with authority and power he commandeth the unclean spirits, and they come out" (Luke 4:18-21, 36).

"And having spoiled principalities and powers [with their deception and destruction], he made a shew of them openly [on the cross], triumphing over them in it" (Colossians 2:15).

"He that committeth sin is of the devil; for the devil sinneth from the beginning. For this purpose the Son of God was manifested, that he might destroy the works of the devil" (1 John 3:8).

"Stand fast therefore in the liberty wherewith Christ hath made us free, and be not entangled again with the yoke of bondage. . . . For, brethren, ye have been called unto liberty; only use not liberty for an occasion to the flesh, but by love serve one another" (Galatians 5:1, 13).

What Can You Do?

Take seriously the bondage in which you are involved. God cares about you and has a solution. Your real problem is not an incurable illness, but sin. And Jesus came to deal with sin (1 Corinthians 6:11). You need to be spiritually reborn and baptized with the Holy Spirit. You need to change your life patterns. You also may need help for deliverance from drugs and healing. Be bold. Take a fearless inventory of your life. Ask for help from your family, Christian friends, a local church pastor, or call Teen Challenge or a local drug hotline.

It is said that it takes thirty-one days to break a habit. Drug addiction is a "life-dominating" problem, so radical changes must be made regarding associates, social atmosphere, places frequented, etc. Replacement, not abstention, is the key. Find a Christian coffeehouse, Bible study and prayer group and a warm church fellowship. One good and faithful Christian friend can help enormously.

You need to keep busy and occupy your mind with new things (Philippians 4:8, 9). Learn to yield yourself to Christ rather than to drugs, old friends, self-pity, guilt, fear, etc.

How to Be Spiritually Reborn

God has a plan for your salvation. Call on the Lord to save you—mind, body and soul (1 John 1:9). Receive Him as your Savior and Lord (John 1:12). Believe Him. He said He would not turn anyone away. He loves you and gave His life for you (John 3:16, 17).

How to Receive the Baptism with the Holy Spirit

Once you become a Christian, you can have God's power available through the Holy Spirit. You will be able to live as God intended

(Ezekiel 36:27). The Holy Spirit empowers you to help others (Acts 1:8), He aids and teaches you (John 14:26; 1 Corinthians 2:13), and guides you into truth (John 16:13) and in life (Acts 10:19; 13:2; 16:6).

You may want to ask someone already baptized with the Holy Spirit to pray with you. Just as you asked the Lord to forgive your sins, believing He would, ask Him now to baptize you with the Holy Spirit (Luke 11:13). He promised to do so, so take Him at His word that He does what you ask. Thank and praise Him for being a God who does as He promises.

Tell someone else what you've done. Other Christians and the church will rejoice with you and help you. The angels rejoice with you. God rejoices with you.

As You Pray

Thank God for His love, concern, and power to save and deliver. Renounce the drugs, old friends, and hangouts connected with your drug problem. Yield yourself to Jesus. Thank Him for coming into your heart and filling you with the Holy Spirit. Take Him at His word and thank Him for delivering you from drugs.

References/Homework

Acts 2:3, 38; 8:17; 10:44; 19:6	The Holy Spirit first experienced
Romans 11:2a	God does not reject His chosen ones
Philippians 4:4-9	Growth in Christ

Begin healing broken relationships by forgiving, and making restitution where necessary.

Set up a plan for Bible reading and quiet prayer time. Go to church. Seek warm Christian fellowship and a group such as Teen Challenge to talk and pray with.

Read *The Cross and the Switchblade,* David Wilkerson; *Run, Baby, Run,* Nicky Cruz.

Notes

ENEMIES

What can you do about your enemies? How can you cope with a person who threatens you or is hostile toward you? God has the answer to these questions.

The Word of God teaches us not to be bitter, hostile or vengeful toward another person. You might not like what others do or say, but you must love them as Christ commanded. Matthew 5:43-48 demonstrates how you should act. Rather than react in retaliation, you are to love those that hate you. Satan is the source of contention (Ephesians 6:12) and would have you make others your enemies. Your fleshly nature allows him the opportunity to deceive you (Galatians 5:19-21). God wants your fleshly nature replaced with His nature, the fruit of the Holy Spirit (Galatians 5:22, 23).

What Scripture Says

"If thou meet thine enemy's ox or his ass going astray, thou shalt surely bring it back to him again. If thou see the ass of him that hateth thee lying under his burden, and wouldest forbear to help him, thou shalt surely help with him" (Exodus 23:4, 5). (Go out of your way to help your enemy.)

"Rejoice not when thine enemy falleth, and let not thine heart be glad when he stumbleth: Lest the Lord see it, and it displease him, and he turn away his wrath from him" (Proverbs 24:17, 18). (Do not rejoice when your enemy is down.)

"But I say unto you which hear, Love your enemies, do good to them which hate you. Bless them that curse you, and pray for them which despitefully use you. And unto him that smiteth thee on the one cheek offer also the other; and him that taketh away thy cloak forbid not to take thy coat also. Give to every man that asketh of thee; and of him that taketh away thy goods ask them not again. And as ye would that men should do to you, do ye also to them likewise.

ENEMIES

For if ye love them which love you, what thank have ye? For sinners also love those that love them. And if ye do good to them which do good to you, what thank have ye? for sinners also do even the same. And if ye lend to them of whom ye hope to receive, what thank have ye? for sinners also lend to sinners, to receive as much again. But love ye your enemies, and do good, and lend, hoping for nothing again; and your reward shall be great, and ye shall be the children of the Highest: for he is kind unto the unthankful and to the evil. Be ye therefore merciful, as your Father also is merciful. Judge not, and ye shall not be judged: condemn not, and ye shall not be condemned: forgive, and ye shall be forgiven" (Luke 6:27-37). (Love your enemies.)

"Bless them which persecute you: bless, and curse not. . . . Dearly beloved, avenge not yourselves, but rather give place unto wrath: for it is written, Vengeance is mine; I will repay, saith the Lord. Therefore if thine enemy hunger, feed him; if he thirst, give him drink: for in so doing thou shalt heap coals of fire on his head. Be not overcome of evil, but overcome evil with good" (Romans 12:14, 19-21).

God's Answer
For God to help you work out your problems, you must first be assured that you have been forgiven for your own sins. Have you asked the Lord to forgive you? If not, do so right now. Repent of all known sin, including any feelings of enmity toward another.

You cannot afford to entertain even the thought of declaring someone your enemy. It will hurt you to harbor hate—which is as the sin of murder—in your heart. For your own physical, emotional, and spiritual well-being, evaluate your feelings and attitudes. Are they Christ-like? Pray for the fruit of the Spirit, which includes love, goodness, kindness, meekness and patience (Galatians 5:22, 23). God will produce love within you that may not have been there before. Ask God to forgive your attitude, especially feelings of bitterness, resentment and hate. Also forgive your enemy and ask God to forgive him.

If possible, go to your former enemy and together confront the conflict between you. Genuinely ask for his forgiveness, no matter what his response or attitude toward you. As you love your enemy, you will gain a new brother in Christ, according to God's Word (Matthew 5:44ff.; Romans 12:17-21). Pray with your new friend and seek ways that you can cultivate genuine friendship.

If your heart is not right toward another, God will not accept your worship. He will honor your relationship with Him as that broken human relationship is corrected (Matthew 7:3-5). You may then ask in good conscience and faith to be baptized with the Holy Spirit (Luke 11:13). The Holy Spirit will help you live a godly, blessed life free from bondage of sin. He will give you love for all—even your former enemies.

As You Pray

Thank God for His love and patience. Admit that your feelings and attitudes have not been Christ-like. Ask Him to forgive you and give you a genuine love for your former enemy. Ask God to forgive your new friend for anything he may have done or said against you. Thank God for giving you love for your friend and for showing you ways to cultivate it. Pray for your friend to be blessed of God and pray that he will be given a great love for you also.

References/Homework

Psalm 23:5	God provides for needs
Matthew 5:44-46	Love your enemies
Psalm 18:47, 48	God is our avenger
Psalm 44:5-7	Victory through God
Proverbs 16:7	God causes enemies to be at peace with us
Philippians 4:13	Strength in Christ promised

Notes

_____

_____

_____

ENVY/JEALOUSY

Do you gossip, backbite, make snide remarks, or try to build yourself up by degrading another? If so, you are guilty of the sin of envy or jealousy. Envy and jealousy are works of the flesh (Galatians 5:21) and a product of the natural sin of self-consciousness or pride.

Sin, when full-blown, produces destruction, tragedy and death (Galatians 5:19-21; James 1:14, 15). So if you are envious or jealous you may soon find yourself beset with undesirable, destructive emotions. You may adopt a judgmental attitude followed by hate. This leads to spiritual murder, character assassination and other sins against those of whom you are envious or jealous.

What Scripture Says

"A sound heart is the life of the flesh: but envy the rottenness of the bones" (Proverbs 14:30).

"For ye are yet carnal: for whereas there is among you envying, and strife, and divisions, are ye not carnal, and walk as men?" (1 Corinthians 3:3).

"Now the works of the flesh are manifest, which are these; Adultery, fornication, uncleanness, lasciviousness, idolatry, witchcraft, hatred, variance, emulations, wrath, strife, seditions, heresies, envyings, murders, drunkenness, revellings, and such like: of the which I tell you before, as I have also told you in time past, that they which do such things shall not inherit the kingdom of God" (Galatians 5:19-21).

"But if ye have bitter *envying* and strife in your hearts, glory not, and lie not against the truth. . . . For where envying and strife is, there is confusion and every evil work" (James 3:14, 16).

"The thief cometh not, but for to steal, and to kill, and to destroy: I am come that they might have life, and that they might have it more abundantly" (John 10:10).

To Be Free

Salvation in Christ includes freedom from the bondage of sin (John 8:36). The baptism of the Holy Spirit opens your life to the abundance and gifts of God. The Holy Spirit produces the virtues and qualities of godliness in you, leaving no place for sin (Galatians 5:22, 23).

You have no reason to be envious. As a Christian, you are a King's kid, an heir to all that is Christ's. God has something better for you than you can imagine (1 Corinthians 2:9).

Worship God in praise. Focus your attention on God (Colossians 3:1-4) rather than your own lack, which leads to envy and jealousy. Affirm that love now prevails in your life and jealousy and envy are dead (1 Corinthians 13:4). Affirm that honesty, not strife and envy, is allowing you to walk in God's love and light (Romans 13:13). And affirm that from this moment, you will seek to walk in the Spirit where there is no provoking of one another and no envy (Galatians 5:25, 26).

Rejoice and be glad when others are blessed or exalted. It pleases God and wins a friend (Romans 12:14-16). In due time, each of us will reap our blessings, if we don't faint and become weary in well-doing.

As You Pray

Pray for forgiveness of your envy/jealousy and to be filled with the Holy Spirit, that you may know and experience the glory of God within you.

Ask God to give you a vision of His glory and love and regard for those toward whom you have been envious and jealous.

Pray for the fruit of the Spirit to be produced within you (Galatians 5:22, 23).

List God's alternative behavior and begin practicing it. Discover God's best for you. Begin to note all the praiseworthy things about the one(s) of whom you were envious or jealous. Share those things with that person(s). You will find a bond of love growing as you begin to see how God sees and loves that person(s).

ENVY/JEALOUSY

References/Homework
1 Timothy 6:6; Proverbs 15:16; Philippians 4:11; Hebrews 13:5;
2 Corinthians 9:8.

Notes

_____

_____

_____

_____

_____

_____

_____

_____

_____

FAITH

Faith is one of the greatest and most necessary of God's gifts. To have faith means that you believe God's Word and then act upon it. Belief plus action equals faith.

Anything less than faith is sin. If you lack faith, it is because you don't fully trust God and His Word. This inability to believe God is probably the sin most common to God's own people.

Faith is a gift (Ephesians 2:8, 9; 1 Corinthians 12:9). It comes to you as you receive God's Word (Romans 10:17). Though small, as the tiniest of seeds, faith will move mountains if exercised.

What Scripture Says

"And Jesus said unto them, Because of your unbelief: for verily I say unto you, If ye have faith as a grain of mustard seed, ye shall say unto this mountain, Remove hence to yonder place; and it shall remove; and nothing shall be impossible unto you" (Matthew 17:20).

"So then faith cometh by hearing, and hearing by the word of God" (Romans 10:17).

"That whosoever believeth in him should not perish, but have eternal life" (John 3:15).

"Therefore being justified by faith, we have peace with God through our Lord Jesus Christ" (Romans 5:1).

"To another faith [is given] by the same Spirit . . ." (1 Corinthians 12:9).

"Knowing that a man is not justified by the works of the law, but by the faith of Jesus Christ, even we have believed in Jesus Christ, that we might be justified by the faith of Christ, and not by the works of the law: for by the works of the law shall no flesh be justified" (Galatians 2:16).

FAITH

Building Faith Muscles

God requires faith in order to be saved. This means that you already have faith. You just need to exercise it.

Knowing God's character can help you confess His Word with confidence. God is loving, faithful, kind, good, merciful and holy. He keeps His promises. He will meet your needs.

If you still have problems believing God, remember that you can "live by the faith" of Christ. He is both full of faith and faithful. He has enough faith for all of us. Ask Him to help you in your unbelief.

Maybe your confession needs an overhaul too. Remember that God's promises are "yea and amen!" In the Kingdom of God everything is positive. In Satan's realm everything is negative. Satan is a liar and a deceiver. Rather than being concerned with the devil, focus on the promises of God. Confess that God's Word is true, just as you confessed the Lord Jesus to receive salvation (Romans 10:9, 10). Remind yourself of faith-building experiences that have taken place in your life and the lives of others. In so doing, God will increase your faith. Seek a church where people believe God and His Word. Let them help you build your faith.

As You Pray

Ask God to give you the gift of faith and answer your prayers. Believe that He will do it. Praise and thank Him for it. As you offer sacrifices of praise, you will discover that God is ministering to you in your need (Hebrews 13:15; Psalm 22:3; Romans 8:28). You will see your faith grow.

References/Homework

Read *New Thresholds of Faith*, Kenneth Hagin; *Real Faith*, Price.

Galatians 2:16	Faith brings righteousness
Ephesians 2:8, 9	Faith is a gift
Ephesians 6:16	Faith is a shield against satanic attacks
James 1:3	Faith brings endurance
1 Peter 1:5	Faith brings blessings

John 5:24	Faith assures eternal life (cf. John 11:25)
John 12:46	Faith dispels darkness
John 20:31	The Word of God brings faith
Romans 10:9, 10	Salvation through faith

Notes

_____

_____

_____

_____

_____

_____

_____

_____

FASTING

Fasting means to withhold food and/or drink from your body in order to be more sensitive to God. In doing this, you empty or deny yourself and "mortify" your flesh.

You may decide to fast because of your personal circumstances, or God Himself may prompt you. Either way, fasting is of no spiritual value unless you do it deliberately, with no desire but to seek God: "I have esteemed the words of his mouth more than my necessary food" (Job 23:12).

There are three basic types of fast:

Absolute—no food or drink

Normal—limited time

Partial—limited diet

What Scripture Says

"When I was gone up into the mount to receive the tables of stone, even the tables of the covenant which the Lord made with you, then I abode in the mount *forty days and forty nights, I neither did eat bread nor drink water*. . . . So I turned and came down from the mount, and the mount burned with fire; and the two tables of the covenant were in my two hands. And I looked, and behold, ye had sinned against the Lord your God, and had made you a molten calf: ye had turned aside quickly out of the way which the Lord commanded you. And I took the two tables, and cast them out of my two hands, and brake them before your eyes. And I fell down before the Lord, as at the first forty days and forty nights: I did neither eat bread, nor drink water, because of all your sins which ye sinned, in doing wickedly in the sight of the Lord to provoke him to anger" (Deuteronomy 9:9, 15-18). *(The extended absolute fast.)* NOTE: This was a supernatural fast. It is not advisable to go beyond 3-7 days without fluids.

". . . being forty days tempted of the devil. And in those days he did eat nothing: and when they were ended, he afterward hungered" (Luke 4:2). *(The extended partial or absolute fast.)*

"And Saul rose from the earth; and when his eyes were opened, he saw no man; but they led him by the hand, and brought him into Damascus. And he was three days without sight, and neither did eat nor drink" (Acts 9:8, 9). *(The normal fast.)*

"But Daniel purposed in his heart that he would not defile himself with the portion of the king's meat, nor with the wine which he drank: therefore he requested of the prince of the eunuchs that he might not defile himself" (Daniel 1:8). *(The partial fast.)*

Examine Your Motives

The Bible stresses the importance of fasting. But it is just as important to know *why* you are fasting (1 Corinthians 4:5).

Jesus tells us that the hypocrites fast to show other people that they are fasting (Matthew 6:16). As Christians, we are called to fast for spiritual purposes in secret (Matthew 6:18).

Your fast should be motivated by a sincere desire to communicate with God. It is a time when you stop and give Him your attention and respond from the heart to His word for you. If you don't do this, your fast may be motivated by self-interest.

Other godly motivations for fasting include intercession for a specific need for yourself or others. For example, you may be fasting on behalf of the nation, its leaders, or the dire circumstances or financial problems of yourself or others for whom you are burdened. Godly motives for fasting are spoken of in Isaiah 58:6, 7.

How to Know God Is Speaking

You may be seeking God's word to you for a particular need. If so, ask God to help you be sensitive to His Spirit during the time of fasting. Be particularly sensitive to Scripture you read, as well as sermons, teachings and anything spoken to you during times of ministry. Take notes, recording any spiritual insights you receive or any revelation on your own status and relation to God. At the conclusion of the fast, look for a theme running through your notes. You may find that God is speaking to you through them.

FASTING

How to Know Your Fast Is Honored

When your sense of burden is lifted, normally that will indicate that your fast should end and God is honoring it. It is assumed that you were serious and determined in your spirit (versus a fleshly, human effort) and/or that your fast was prompted by the Holy Spirit.

If you were fasting for a particular need, expect some indication that the circumstances for which you fasted are changing. Keep in mind that a seemingly unrelated circumstance may occur which will ultimately change the immediate ones. Thank and praise God for all you observe, hear, read and experience: "For we know that all things work together for good to them that love God, to them who are the called according to his purpose" (Romans 8:28).

Expect to find that your fast was edifying to you personally as well as beneficial to whomever or whatever you were fasting for. The results of a chosen fast of God are shown in Isaiah 58:8ff.

References/Homework

Read *The Adventures of Fasting*, James Beall; *God's Chosen Fast*, Arthur Wallis.

Isaiah 58	Motive and reward of fasting
Acts 13:2, 3; 14:23	Fasting and God's commission to serve
Joel 1:14; 2:12	Fasting enjoined
Matthew 6:17, 18; 17:21	Fast privately

Notes

_____

_____

_____

_____

_____

_____

FAVOR

One of the principles of the Kingdom of God is that God favors a just man (Proverbs 12:2). As God's child, you can be assured of favor with God and man. God has promised you victory over bad experiences, fear, and negativism. He has also promised to meet your most pressing needs.

Jesus said that He came so that you might have a full, meaningful, purposeful, abundant life (John 10:10b). God's favor is "yea and amen" in every promise of His Word.

What Scripture Says

"But thou, O Lord, art a God full of compassion, and gracious, long-suffering, and plenteous in mercy and truth" (Psalm 86:15).

"And Jesus said unto them, Because of your unbelief: for verily I say unto you, If you have faith as a grain of mustard seed, ye shall say unto this mountain, Remove hence to yonder place; and it shall remove; and nothing shall be impossible unto you" (Matthew 17:20).

"But the Lord was with Joseph, and shewed him mercy, and gave him favour in the sight of the keeper of the prison" (Genesis 39:21).

"Wait on the Lord: be of good courage, and he shall strengthen thine heart: wait, I say, on the Lord" (Psalm 27:14).

"If any man serve me, him will my Father honour [favor]" (John 12:26b).

"I love them that love me; and those that seek me early shall find me. Riches and honour [favor] are with me; yea, durable riches and righteousness" (Proverbs 8:17, 18).

How Favor Is Received

The Bible contains many benedictions which ask that God's face would shine upon you. The Bible also says that God causes even your enemies to be at peace with you (Proverbs 16:7).

FAVOR

You believe in your heart and confess with your mouth (Romans 10:10). That which comes from your mouth—the words, confessions, denials and doubts that you utter—can defile you (Matthew 15:18). Or, your confession can turn the tide from defeat to victory. If God says you have favor, you must confess it even in the face of impossible odds in order to receive it.

Make a list of all God's promises pertaining to your concerns, whether you need a job, have marriage difficulties, or whatever. Begin to confess God's favor according to the promises. God's promises are "yea and amen" (2 Corinthians 1:20).

As a child of God, you can confess that God's grace will be upon you and that you will flourish and prosper (Proverbs 14:11; Psalm 84:11; 92:12).

However, God requires that you do not regard iniquity in your heart. Otherwise He will not hear you (Psalm 66:18). If you have not called on the Lord to forgive you of your sins, do so now. God wants you to experience His salvation and baptism with the Spirit so that you will be eligible and equipped for all He has for you.

You can ask a Christian friend or your pastor to pray with you and to seek the Lord for further discernment regarding your needs. You may have deep problems that need to be resolved before you confess and receive God's favor.

Favor from God comes because of His love and grace. God does not bless out of obligation, but out of love. In claiming and professing His favor, you are recognizing this and you should thank Him accordingly. It is also important to be in agreement with God who promises His favor.

As You Pray
Praise and thank God for His favor upon you. Rebuke fear, doubt, and faithlessness. Receive, in the name of Jesus, God's favor upon you.

Reference/Homework
Read *Favor, The Road to Success,* Bob Buess, Box 959, Van, TX 75790.

FAVOR

Begin to change your thinking. To be transformed, you need your mind renewed. Search the Scriptures, using a concordance, for God's word on His favorable promises to you. Practice confessing them.

Notes

_____

_____

_____

_____

_____

_____

_____

_____

FEAR

Fear is an often strong emotion caused by the anticipation of danger, trouble or evil. Fear also may result from an embarrassing or unpleasant experience. You may fear being exposed to the experience again or meeting someone involved in the incident.

To be afraid (filled with fear) is to lack trust in God. The Bible says fear has torment and he that fears is not made perfect in love. If you are fearful (full of fear), it is because you do not believe God, who promises deliverance from fear. Your fearfulness is a sin.

On the other hand, you are to "fear" God. This means you must revere Him, and with a sense of awe, honor and respect Him. Whatever the need, He will be with you in every circumstance (Psalm 23).

What Scripture Says
"I sought the Lord, and he heard me, and delivered me from all my fears" (Psalm 34:4).

"There is no fear in love: but perfect love casteth out fear: because fear hath torment. He that feareth is not made perfect in love" (1 John 4:18).

"For God hath not given us the spirit of fear; but of power, and of love, and of a sound mind" (2 Timothy 1:7).

"The Lord is my light and my salvation; whom shall I fear? the Lord is the strength of my life; of whom shall I be afraid?" (Psalm 27:1).

"Fear thou not; for I am with thee: be not dismayed; for I am thy God: I will strengthen thee; yea, I will help thee; yea, I will uphold thee with the right hand of my righteousness" (Isaiah 41:10).

"Ye that fear the Lord, praise him; all ye the seed of Jacob, glorify him; and fear him, all ye the seed of Israel" (Psalm 22:23).

"I will bless the Lord at all times: his praise shall continually be in my mouth. . . . The angel of the Lord encampeth round about them that fear him and delivereth them" (Psalm 34:1, 7).

"He that dwelleth in the secret place of the most High shall abide under the shadow of the Almighty. . . . A thousand shall fall at thy side, and ten thousand at thy right hand; but it shall not come nigh thee" (Psalm 91:1, 7).

How to Be Free

Call on the Lord in prayer. Accept His invitation to save you from all sin. Invite Him to be Lord of your life. He is Lord of fear just as He is Lord of all things. You need the ability to overcome all sin, whether fear or any other temptation or attack you face as a child of God. Ask the Lord to baptize you with the Holy Spirit and power (Luke 11:13; Acts 1:8). With new Holy Spirit boldness, you can chase the devil away rather than being overcome by your fear.

Fear is something that you feel and do that God commanded you not to do. It is sin. Learn to affirm your faith in God. Confess the truths of Scripture out loud (Psalm 27:1; 2 Timothy 1:7).

Ask your pastor, a Christian counselor, or other Holy Spirit-filled Christian to agree with you in prayer for boldness in Christ. There is freedom from fear in Christ. Repent of being fearful. Repent of any resentment and bitterness you may feel toward anyone whom you fear. Ask God to give you love for them instead. Love will replace the fear.

The best way to combat fear is to gain, and promote within yourself, a reverence for God. Begin offering praise (honor and respect) to God. He will dispel all fear and minister faith in its place. Praise Him who surrounds you with His angels (Psalm 34).

As You Pray

In agreement with a prayer partner, bind the spirit of fear and torment in the name of Jesus. Receive God's peace and rest. Thank the Father for sending the Holy Spirit to minister to you, and for restoring your confidence in the promises of His Word. Join with your prayer partner in praise and thanksgiving, honoring and revering God. Agree with God's Word that He delivers and saves all who call upon Him.

FEAR

References/Homework

Genesis 15:1; 26:24; 46:3	God is a shield against fear
Exodus 14:13, 14	God fights our battles
Joshua 1:9	God is ever present
Judges 6:10	Godless nations are no threat to God's people
Matthew 10:26, 28	Boldness enjoined
Luke 8:50	Faith dispels fear
Acts 27:24	Assurance in face of death
Deuteronomy 28	Obedience brings blessing
Hebrews 13:5, 6	God does not abandon us
Psalm 23:4; 34:4	God delivers from fear
1 John 4:18	Love drives out fear
2 Timothy 1:7	The Spirit of God fills with power, love, and self-control
Psalm 27:1	Strength promised
Isaiah 41:10	Strength promised

Notes

_____

_____

_____

_____

_____

_____

_____

_____

_____

_____

FINANCES

The wealth of the world is God's (Psalm 50:10). He has it available for those who have called upon Him for salvation.

If you are struggling with financial burdens, take heart. God has promised to meet all your needs if you are a child of His and living according to His righteousness (Matthew 6:33). Furthermore, if you are faithful in your tithing and giving of offerings, He has promised to give you an overabundance of blessing (Malachi 3:8-10).

What Scripture Says

"But seek ye first the kingdom of God, and his righteousness; and all these things shall be added unto you" (Matthew 6:33).

"Will a man rob God? Yet ye have robbed me. But ye say, Wherein have we robbed thee? In tithes and offerings. Ye are cursed with a curse: for ye have robbed me, even this whole nation. Bring ye all the tithes into the storehouse, that there may be meat in mine house, and prove me now herewith, saith the Lord of hosts, if I will not open you the windows of heaven, and pour you out a blessing, that there shall not be room enough to receive it" (Malachi 3:8-10).

"But I have all, and abound; I am full, having received of Epaphroditus the things which were sent from you, an odour of a sweet smell, a sacrifice acceptable, well-pleasing to God. But my God shall supply all your need according to his riches in glory by Jesus Christ" (Philippians 4:18, 19).

God's Best for You

To receive financial blessings, you must obey God (Malachi 3:8-10). His blessings of financial health for you may be stopped because of disobedience. In fact, your greatest need may be spiritual rather than financial. Ask Him if there is something lacking in your life. Seek to know His will for your life. Trust Him to meet all your needs.

FINANCES

If you are a Christian who seems to be in God's will, but you are still experiencing financial problems, seek God for knowledge or wisdom regarding the situation. The Bible tells us we will reap in due time if we don't faint along the way.

Satan may have your financial blessings bound, as with Job, so that you can't receive them. Bind Satan and call on God to send ministering angels (Hebrews 1:14). Command Satan to loose God's blessings.

Fasting may be the instrument you need to loose yokes and break bonds. See Isaiah 58:6, 7 for the motives for fasting.

It is also possible that God is reordering your vocation or some other aspect of your life. He may be using financial problems in the reordering process.

As You Pray
Seek God's word for you at this time. Offer thanks and praise in agreement with God according to Matthew 18:19. Praise and thank God for His favor toward you.

References/Homework
Read *Seed Faith,* Oral Roberts; *How to Live Like a King's Kid,* Harold Hill.

Matthew 6:33	Doing God's righteousness
Proverbs 3:5, 6	Acknowledging Him
Revelation 1:6	Recognizing your status
Luke 6:38	Give and it shall be given unto you

Do a study in the Bible regarding finances, knowing God's will and righteous occupations.

Also see:

Psalm 37:4, 5	Heart's desire promised
Joshua 1:8	Prosperity promised
2 Corinthians 9:6, 7	We reap as we plant
Mark 11:23, 24	Faith enjoined

FORGIVENESS

If you have ever experienced feelings of guilt, you need to know that forgiveness is available to you, that you can feel "clean" again. The different aspects of forgiveness are: 1) God's forgiveness, which is necessary for salvation and His favor toward you; 2) your forgiveness of others, necessary for your own health and to release others to receive God's favor; and 3) self-forgiveness, also necessary for your own health spiritually, mentally and physically.

To love the Lord with all your heart, mind, soul and strength and your neighbor as yourself is to have experienced forgiveness and to have forgiven others as well as yourself. See the Lord's Prayer, Matthew 6:12.

What Scripture Says

"He hath not dealt with us after our sins; nor rewarded us according to our iniquities. For as the heaven is high above the earth, so great is his mercy toward them that fear him. As far as the east is from the west, so far hath he removed our transgressions from us" (Psalm 103:10-12).

"I, even I, am he that blotteth out thy transgressions for mine own sake, and will not remember thy sins" (Isaiah 43:25).

"For if ye forgive men their trespasses, your heavenly Father will also forgive you" (Matthew 6:14).

"If we say that we have no sin, we deceive ourselves, and the truth is not in us. If we confess our sins, he is faithful and just to forgive us our sins, and to cleanse us from all unrighteousness" (1 John 1:8, 9).

"And when he had said this, he breathed on them, and saith unto them, Receive ye the Holy Ghost: Whose soever sins ye remit, they are remitted unto them; and whose soever sins ye retain, they are retained" (John 20:22, 23).

FORGIVENESS

God's Forgiveness

The greatest joy ever known and the greatest love ever experienced is when a person is forgiven and cleansed of his sin. The Bible says the angels rejoice when one sinner repents. Even if you were the only person who ever lived, Jesus would have died for you that you could be forgiven.

"If your life has no joy in it, no victory in it or no happiness in it, I know why," said a famous preacher of the past. "It is because you have not repented." Even if you are a Christian already, be open to the Holy Spirit revealing unconfessed and unforsaken sin. Take seriously your feelings of guilt. Sins must be repented of.

A young soldier felt sullied after committing his first crimson sin. In despair he cried, "How can I ever face my mother? I would give anything in the world to just feel clean again." You may have similar feelings of shame and remorse. Yet God said there is forgiveness in Jesus. "Though your sins be as scarlet, they shall be as white as snow; though red like crimson, they shall be as wool" (Isaiah 1:18).

"Oh, what manner of love the Father has given to us, that we should be called the sons of God!" Forgiveness is yours. Call on Him. Ask Him to forgive. Receive His forgiveness. It is yours when you repent.

Is there some reason why you do not feel free in your spirit? Could it be that you are harboring unforgiveness toward someone whom you feel has wronged you? To harbor unforgiveness is to hate. And in His Word, God likens hate to the sin of murder.

No matter how you were wronged, all that holding a grudge will do for you is to bring about emotional distress, anguish, hate, bitterness, physical illness and a general feeling of unhappiness resulting in spiritual bankruptcy. It is God's business to judge and to bring revenge. You need not labor under a burden that is not yours, nor a responsibility that belongs to God.

If you can get no relief from your burden of guilt, take a fearless and bold inventory of yourself. Do you need to forgive and ask God to forgive some person? When forgiven, the other person is released from the bondage of the condemnation you have heaped on him (Acts 7:60). What you bind is bound. What you loose is loosed (John 20:22,

90

23). When you let go of your bitterness and resentment, God will be free to work with the person toward whom you held these feelings. And you will know release and joy.

God wants you to be free. After you have forgiven you will experience freedom. It is not worth your spiritual, emotional or physical health to bear the burden of unforgiveness. If possible, tell the person for whom you have carried a grudge that you forgive, and have asked God to forgive, him. May God help you forgive.

Forgiveness of Self

After knowing God has forgiven, and after forgiving others from whom you have experienced wrong, there should be no barrier to being able to forgive yourself. By faith, accept God's Word in Isaiah 43:18, 19. Begin to minister honor and respect to God who is doing a new thing in you, by offering sacrifices of praise to Him (Hebrews 13:15).

Satan will try to accuse you still, but resist him. Praise to God (exalting God) will cause Satan to flee from you. There is no condemnation for those who are in Christ Jesus. You are free (Romans 8:1, 2).

As You Pray

Pray that you will receive the fruit of the Spirit, love, joy, peace, goodness, kindness, faithfulness, meekness, patience and self-control. Thank and praise God for delivering you from any oppressive spirit which would prevent you from receiving the fruit of the Spirit. Thank God for His anointing upon you, and rejoice in praises to Him for His great love and mercy to you and others.

References/Homework

Forgive and be forgiven:
Matthew 6:14
Mark 11:25, 26
Ephesians 4:32
Isaiah 43:25
John 20:22, 23

Forgive self:
Isaiah 43:18, 19
Philippians 3:13
1 John 1:9
Jeremiah 18:4 (you are being made into a new vessel)

FORGIVENESS

Colossians 3:13
Matthew 18:21, 22
Galatians 6:1, 2

Also see:
Acts 7:60 (Stephen's prayer that no sin be charged to his slayers)
Hebrews 8:12
Colossians 3:12, 13
1 John 2:1, 2
Galatians 5:19-23

Read *The Freedom of Forgiveness* by David Augsburger, Moody Press.

Notes

_____

_____

_____

_____

_____

_____

_____

_____

FREEDOM FROM DEMON BONDAGE

Demon bondage can be brought about when an individual is possessed, oppressed, or is in rebellion toward God (sins of the flesh). It takes God's discernment to determine which of these is producing the bondage in an individual's life.

The Bible makes it clear that there are demons, or evil spirits, in the world that interfere in people's lives (Ephesians 6:11-19). Evil forces or powers influence and control the minds of individuals, bring sickness and cause undesirable behavior, inability to function normally, and even suicide. As a result of these forces, people can become a danger to themselves as well as others.

What Scripture Says

"There shall not be found among you any one that maketh his son or his daughter to pass through the fire, or that useth divination, or an observer of times, or an enchanter, or a witch, or a charmer, or a consulter with familiar spirits, or a wizard, or a necromancer. For all that do these things are an abomination unto the Lord: and because of these abominations the Lord thy God doth drive them out from before thee" (Deuteronomy 18:10-13).

"For we wrestle not against flesh and blood, but against principalities, against powers, against rulers of the darkness of this world, against spiritual wickedness in high places" (Ephesians 6:12).

". . . there met him two possessed with devils, coming out of the tombs, exceeding fierce, so that no man might pass by that way. . . . And he said unto them, Go. And when they were come out, they went into the herd of swine: and, behold, the whole herd of swine ran violently down a steep place into the sea, and perished in the waters" (Matthew 8:28b, 32).

FREEDOM FROM DEMON BONDAGE

"There came also a multitude out of the cities round about unto Jerusalem, bringing sick folks, and them with which were vexed with unclean spirits: and they were healed every one" (Acts 5:16).

"Now the works of the flesh are manifest, which are these; Adultery, fornication, uncleanness, lasciviousness, idolatry, witchcraft, hatred, variance, emulations, wrath, strife, seditions, heresies, envyings, murders, drunkenness, revellings, and such like: of the which I tell you before, as I have also told you in time past, that they which do such things shall not inherit the kingdom of God" (Galatians 5:19-21).

Indications of Demon Activity

The following areas may help you to recognize your need for being released from demonic oppression, possession or bondages of the flesh (sin):

1. Compulsion to abuse animals or people;
2. Sexual perversion and immorality (homosexuality, molestation, etc.);
3. A compulsion to abuse your body (drugs, alcohol, gluttony, abuse or misuse of other substances, etc.);
4. Seeking spiritual knowledge through Eastern religions and other counterfeit religious groups (TM, yoga, humanism, etc.);
5. Involvement in occult practices (fortune-telling, Satanism, etc.);
6. Mental distress or oppression (anxiety, fear, anger, disorientation, etc.);
7. Psychological disorders (split and multiple personalities, paranoia, etc.);
8. Physical disorders may be demon caused (Matthew 9:32, 33);
9. Lack of freedom or joy in the Lord (spiritual bondage);
10. Inability or constant refusal to repent of sin, though you know you are sinning (rebellion).

See Bible passages under References/Homework and in a Bible dictionary and concordance for examples of the above. If you are having difficulty in discerning your problem, please seek help from a local pastor, elder, or Christian counselor who will help you to discern your need and can counsel and pray with you.

FREEDOM FROM DEMON BONDAGE

What Is God's Answer?

"The Spirit of the Lord is upon me, because he hath anointed me to preach the gospel to the poor; he hath sent me to heal the broken-hearted, to preach deliverance to the captives, and recovering of sight to the blind, to set at liberty them that are bruised. To preach the acceptable year of the Lord" (Luke 4:18, 19).

This prophecy concerning the Messiah was fulfilled in Christ, and the authority noted herein has been passed on to Christians (Mark 16:17).

Jesus came to free those under demon bondage. "For whosoever shall call upon the name of the Lord shall be saved" (Romans 10:13). The term "saved" or "salvation" includes your spiritual, physical and mental health.

You need to pray sincerely to the Lord that He will forgive your sin, cleanse you, be your Savior and Lord and baptize (fill) you with the Holy Spirit (1 John 1:8, 9; John 1:12; Luke 11:13; Acts 1:8). The Holy Spirit will give you the power to overcome demon bondage, activity and influence. You will be free. You can experience an abundant, full, meaningful life with the joy and purpose God desires for you (John 10:10).

If You Can't Pray in Victory

First, you need to be sure your problem is not a fleshly, willful one on your part. Take a bold, fearless inventory of yourself. You must choose whom you will serve: self and fleshly desires, Satan or God? Repent of all sinful desires. Renounce sin and sinfulness and its ingrained habits. Commit yourself to Christ with determination and resolve. After you have repented and asked for forgiveness, accept God's assurance that you are a child of God and have been forgiven.

If you need further help, the elders of the church can pray and minister to you (James 5:14, 15).

How You Can Stay Free

You cannot reckon an evil spirit dead nor crucify an evil spirit. Neither can you cast out the flesh. You must crucify the flesh (Galatians 2:20) and its desires and cast out evil spirits (James 4:7). When demons or evil spirits are cast out, you need something to replace them, lest they return (Matthew 12:43-48).

You can be assured of victory over demons if you have received Jesus as Savior and Lord (John 1:12), and have received the baptism with the Holy Spirit (Acts 1:8). The Holy Spirit guides you into truth, empowers you and intercedes for you. He also gives you spiritual gifts, such as discerning of spirits, for your welfare and that of others (1 Corinthians 12; Mark 16:9-20).

As you receive God's nature, the traits of your fleshly nature (such as irresponsible behavior, pride and lack of love) will be replaced by the fruit of the Spirit (Galatians 5:22, 23).

Your greatest need is to continually study God's Word. Meditate upon the Bible day and night (Joshua 1:8) to put on the whole armor of God that you might be able to effectively overcome the forces of evil (Ephesians 6:10-18). Jesus answered Satan with the Word of God (Luke 4:1-13). You can do the same. Pray without ceasing (1 Thessalonians 5:17) and get into a local church fellowship for further ministry (Hebrews 10:25).

As You Pray
Consistently honor God with thanksgiving and praise. As you give Him first place in your thoughts and actions, Satan and his demons will have no place in your life.

References/Homework
Read *Defeated Enemies,* Corrie Ten Boom; *Demons in the World Today,* Merrill Unger; *The Devil's Alphabet,* Kurt Koch; *His Infernal Majesty,* Dave Breese; *Demons,* Lester Sumrall.

Bible references to demonic activity:
1 Samuel 28
Matthew 8:28-32; 9:32, 33; 12:43-45; 15:22, 28; 17:15-18
Mark 1:23-27
Luke 8:2; 10:17
Acts 5:16; 8:7; 19:12
Revelation 16:13, 14

FRUIT OF THE SPIRIT

The fruit of the Spirit are the virtues of love, joy, peace, patience, kindness, goodness, faithfulness, humility, and self-control. When you display irresponsible behavior, pride, expressions of enmity, lack of love and other works of the flesh (Galatians 5:19-21), you are lacking the fruit of the Spirit.

As a child of God, you are eligible to receive the things of the Spirit of God. You must be willing to let the Holy Spirit produce these virtues within you (Galatians 5:22, 23).

What Scripture Says

"But the Spirit produces love, joy, peace, patience, kindness, goodness, faithfulness, humility, and self-control. There is no law against such things as these" (Galatians 5:22, 23, TEV).

"This I say then, Walk in the Spirit, and ye shall not fulfill the lust of the flesh. . . . If we live in the Spirit, let us also walk in the Spirit" (Galatians 5:16, 25).

"If ye love me, keep my commandments. . . . He that hath my commandments, and keepeth them, he it is that loveth me: and he that loveth me shall be loved of my Father, and I will love him, and will manifest myself to him" (John 14:15, 21).

"And he shall be like a tree planted by the rivers of water, that bringeth forth his fruit in his season; his leaf also shall not wither; and whatsoever he doeth shall prosper" (Psalm 1:3).

How to Receive the Fruit of the Spirit

In the life of the Christian there is a law at work which is the law of the Spirit of life in Christ Jesus (Romans 8:2). When you submit to and apply this law in your life the Holy Spirit can begin to manifest the fruit of the Spirit within you (Romans 8:4).

As a Christian, you should seek the fruit of the Spirit, which is the nature of Jesus being produced within you. Scripture makes it clear

FRUIT OF THE SPIRIT

that total surrender to Christ and His Word opens the way to the life of fruitfulness and spiritual productivity. You should put into action in practical ways the admonition given in Ephesians 4:21-24, to rid yourself of all old deceitful desires, attitudes, practices, etc. Your body is the temple of the Holy Spirit who works within you to present you blameless and holy unto the Lord.

It is important to understand that the Holy Spirit produces the fruit or qualities of the Spirit (Galatians 5:22). How does the Spirit do this? You can find the answer by studying all Bible references which relate to the fruit of the Spirit. For example, see Isaiah 26:3 about "peace" and Romans 5:3 about "patience."

When God commands you to love Him and your neighbor, this is in a very real sense a promise that the Holy Spirit will produce that love within you. Yet there are practical steps you can take to allow Him to do this. Select someone whom you should genuinely love, but don't. Now ask God to give you a great love for that person. Then ask Him to show you how you can bless him or her.

As you are waiting on the Lord to give you a genuine regard for the person, begin to list all his or her good qualities. The more praiseworthy things you discover, the more aware you will become of what God sees in that individual. The more you are aware of what God sees, the more you will find yourself rejoicing with love for that person. Be sure to tell the person of your experience. Share the praiseworthy things you have discovered.

As you receive love, you will also receive the other fruit of the Spirit, including goodness, kindness, meekness (humble submissiveness to God) and faithfulness toward the person and toward God. Jesus says that when you have done something for one of His, you have done it for Him. The fruit of the Spirit are such that when you have them in you, no one can find a reason to accuse you before God. You will find yourself able to get along with other people, and other people able to get along with you.

As You Pray
Ask God to reveal any sin in you. Repent. He will cleanse you of that hindering sin. Then you should ask for the fruit of the Spirit.

98

FRUIT OF THE SPIRIT

Commit yourself to a life in the Spirit, who will reveal practical ways you can obey Him and use your God-given abilities to mature spiritually (Hebrews 5:14). This process is a result of your obedience and commitment to the lordship of Jesus Christ. Praise and thank God for the grace that allows you to become like Jesus and have His qualities.

References/Homework

John 12:24   Death to self insures fruit
Galatians 6:7, 8   We reap in the same realm of our
                         sowing
Ephesians 5:8, 9   Fruit is a product of God's light

Psalm 1, John 15, Psalm 92:13, 14 and James 1:21-25 are all recommended reading.

Notes

_____

_____

_____

_____

_____

_____

_____

_____

_____

THE FULL
COUNSEL OF GOD

Few Christians ever progress in their life in Christ to any degree of spiritual maturity. But when Jesus said, "I am come that they might have life, and that they might have it more abundantly" (John 10:10), He was expressing God's desire that we should become all that we can be in Christ Jesus.

What Scripture Says

"For whosoever shall call upon the name of the Lord shall be saved" (Romans 10:13).

"But ye shall receive power, after that the Holy Ghost is come upon you: and ye shall be witnesses unto me both in Jerusalem, and in all Judaea, and in Samaria, and unto the uttermost part of the earth" (Acts 1:8).

"If ye then, being evil, know how to give good gifts unto your children: how much more shall your heavenly Father give the Holy Spirit to them that ask him?" (Luke 11:13).

"And he gave some, apostles; and some, prophets; and some, evangelists; and some, pastors and teachers; For the perfecting of the saints, for the work of the ministry, for the edifying of the body of Christ" (Ephesians 4:11, 12).

"Put on the whole armour of God, that ye may be able to stand against the wiles of the devil" (Ephesians 6:11).

"But the fruit of the Spirit is love, joy, peace, longsuffering, gentleness, goodness, faith, meekness, temperance: against such there is no law" (Galatians 5:22, 23).

"But the manifestation of the Spirit is given to every man to profit withal. For to one is given . . . the word of wisdom; to another the word of knowledge . . . to another faith . . . to another the gifts of healing . . . to another the working of miracles; to another prophecy;

to another discerning of spirits; to another divers kinds of tongues; to another the interpretation of tongues" (1 Corinthians 12:7-10).

The Overcoming Life

You can have an overcoming, victorious life because of the shed blood of Jesus and because of what you can become in Christ (Revelation 12:10, 11).

The Bible says that as you think in your heart, so have you become (Proverbs 23:7). You will think in a godly way as you receive the full counsel of God (Acts 20:27). As you grow in spiritual knowledge and experience, you will gain spiritual maturity and the abundant life that God promised (3 John 2).

What Is the Full Counsel of God?

Be born again (John 3:3, 5). Receive the baptism with the Holy Spirit (Luke 11:13). Put on God's armor (Ephesians 6:11-17). Ask for and receive the fruit of the Holy Spirit (Galatians 5:22, 23). Grow under the ministry of the Church's apostles, prophets, evangelists, pastors and teachers (Ephesians 4:11, 12). Witness to God and minister to others as you receive the gifts of the Holy Spirit to do so (Romans 12:3-9; 1 Corinthians 12:7-10; 1 Peter 4:10). Learn and practice the principles of the Kingdom of God. As you develop in these essential areas, you will find yourself experiencing the fullness of God's best for you.

How to Receive God's Fullness

I. Be born again. Death reigns over us from our birth (Romans 5:12) because of our sinful nature of self-consciousness versus God-consciousness (1 John 2:16). We think and behave after the lusts (appetites) of our flesh and our eyes, and after the dictates of the pride of life (Galatians 5:19-21).

Jesus came to change your relationship with God (John 3:16). As you pray, confess and repent of your sins. He will save, cleanse and forgive you. And He will give you power (authority) to become a son of God (Romans 10:13; 1 John 1:9; John 1:12.) Have you received Him into your heart and life as Savior and Lord? If not, do so now.

THE FULL COUNSEL OF GOD

II. Baptism with the Holy Spirit. After you have been saved (or born again, adopted, redeemed, converted—all terms describing the experience of salvation) you will find you need power to live the Christian life. This power is available when you are baptized with the Holy Spirit. The Holy Spirit will comfort, guide, help and empower you (Luke 11:13; Joel 2:28-32; John 14 and 16; Acts 1:8; Mark 16:16-20).

Through the Holy Spirit, your experiences will be similar to those of the first disciples. And, yes, you will be able to pray and glorify God in praise, and prophesy in a language you have not learned (Mark 16:17; Acts 2:4, 11; 10:44-47; 1 Corinthians 14:24a and others).

You can pray alone and receive the baptism with the Holy Spirit (Luke 11:13). Or a Spirit-filled friend, pastor, or others in your church can pray with you and help you in your understanding of the Holy Spirit.

III. The fruit of the Spirit. As the Holy Spirit edifies your spirit, you can begin replacing your worldly, fleshly nature with God's nature (Galatians 5:22, 23). Receiving the character traits of God is perhaps the most important need a Christian has. The Holy Spirit will work in every experience and detail of your life to produce the fullness of the nature of God (the fruit of the Spirit).

It is important to draw close to God and earnestly ask Him for the fruit of the Spirit. You do not automatically receive them just because you are a Christian.

IV. Ministries of the Spirit. God has set in the Church five gifted ministries: apostles (missionaries who are sent to preach the gospel and establish churches); prophets (who proclaim God's written or newly revealed, prophetic word to the Church); evangelists (who proclaim His righteousness, holiness, mercy, love, etc., and who call people to turn from sinfulness to repentance); and pastors and teachers (providing spiritual aid and nurture). For you to be spiritually built up in the Lord (Ephesians 4:11-13), it is important that you attend a church fellowship regularly where these ministries are present.

V. God's armor. God's armor is: truth, righteousness, the gospel of peace, faith, salvation and God's Word (your weapon). It is received, put on, and put to use as a result of knowing God's Word. Then, like a soldier, you must maintain your equipment (spiritual armor and arms) through Bible study, the ministry of the church and diligent prayer (Ephesians 6:11-18). With God's armor you can stand against spiritual wickedness in all its forms whether in the physical or spiritual realm.

VI. Gifts of the Spirit. Every Christian has a spiritual gift (not necessarily supernatural) of some kind, depending on his faith (1 Peter 4:10; Romans 12:3-9, "motivational gifts"). The baptism with the Holy Spirit makes you eligible for the supernatural gifts of the Spirit to be manifested through you as you do the works of Christ (John 14:12). This includes overcoming sin, sickness and evil, and ministering to others (2 Corinthians 10:4, 5). Every Spirit-filled Christian can minister through the supernatural gifts (1 Corinthians 12:7-10, 27-31).

VII. Kingdom principles. In practicing the principles of God's Kingdom, you can receive the fulfillment of God's promises. One or more of the following principles will apply to most or all problems you will ever encounter. Become thoroughly familiar with and practice them for victory and growth in your life.

1. Praise to God. He honors those who honor Him (1 Samuel 2:30b). Honor God, the Problem Solver, rather than honoring a problem, sin, temptation, illness, etc.

2. Agreement with God (His Word). The place of agreement is the place of power (Matthew 18:19). Disagreement brings only defeat.

3. Reciprocity. As you give, it will be given in return, in even greater measure (Luke 6:38). As you do for others and for God, it will be done for you.

4. Favor. God favors a just man. He honors those who serve Him (John 12:26). Learn to serve God and walk in His favor.

5. Fasting. Desire to hear from God more than you desire food

to eat (Job 23:12). If you fast in behalf of another, or for your own need, God's reward to you will include healing, personal recognition, protection, favor and His sure guidance (Isaiah 58:6-12).

6. Intercession. To intercede means to stand up for those in need, as a friend or defender (Isaiah 59:16). God acts in response to the prayers of a Christian.

In summary, be satisfied with nothing less than God's full counsel for you. As a maturing, equipped Christian, you will be an overcomer in the world and able to teach others as well.

As You Pray

Thank and praise God daily as you learn, meditate and grow in the basic areas of God's full counsel. Pray for others you know who need to know God's fullness in their lives. Pray for opportunity to speak to them.

References/Homework

Daily, read the Psalms and Proverbs for worship experiences and wisdom.

Notes

_____

_____

_____

_____

_____

_____

_____

_____

_____

_____

GIFTS OF THE SPIRIT

The gifts of the Spirit are supernatural endowments for service and are given according to the character of the ministry that is to be fulfilled. The purpose of all gifts is the same: to edify the body. We should first seek Jesus, the "Giver" of the Holy Spirit and the gifts. The Bible tells us to covet earnestly the best gifts (1 Corinthians 12:31). Through the working of the Holy Spirit, we who believe on Christ are promised to do greater works than He did while ministering on earth (John 14:12). As Christians, the Holy Spirit dwells within us. He teaches us all things and brings the things the Lord teaches us to our remembrance (John 16:7-11, 13-15).

What Scripture Says

"But ye shall receive power, after that the Holy Ghost is come upon you: and ye shall be witnesses unto me . . ." (Acts 1:8).

"Having then gifts differing according to the grace that is given to us, whether prophecy, let us prophesy according to the proportion of faith; or ministry, let us wait on our ministering: or he that teacheth, on teaching; or he that exhorteth, on exhortation: he that giveth, let him do it with simplicity; he that ruleth, with diligence; he that sheweth mercy, with cheerfulness" (Romans 12:6-8).

"Now concerning spiritual gifts, brethren, I would not have you ignorant. . . . Now there are diversities of gifts, but the same Spirit. And there are differences of administrations, but the same Lord. And there are diversities of operations, but it is the same God which worketh all in all" (1 Corinthians 12:1, 4-6).

"But the manifestation of the Spirit is given to every man to profit withal. For to one is given by the Spirit the word of wisdom; to another the word of knowledge by the same Spirit; to another faith by the same Spirit; to another the gifts of healing by the same Spirit;

to another the working of miracles; to another prophecy; to another discerning of spirits; to another divers kinds of tongues; to another the interpretation of tongues: But all these worketh that one and the selfsame Spirit, dividing to every man severally as he will" (1 Corinthians 12:7-11).

"As every man hath received the gift, even so minister the same one to another, as good stewards of the manifold grace of God" (1 Peter 4:10).

Spiritual Matters

The apostle Paul wrote to the Corinthian church about spiritual gifts or "matters" as the Greek word would literally be translated (1 Corinthians 12:1, 4-6). He listed three categories: 1) gifts, 2) administrations (different kinds of service), and 3) operations (different workings). God works all things through Christ, whom He has made Head of the Church. The Holy Spirit distributes the gifts to people who do the works of God.

Gifts of the Spirit are not the same as natural talents or abilities, which are certainly gifts from God. Our talents and abilities allow each of us to contribute to society in a meaningful way. As each person "works" his talent, everyone benefits.

The Supernatural Manifestation Gifts

The supernatural manifestations of the Holy Spirit are worked through each person as the Spirit wills (1 Corinthians 12:8-11). In the history of the Church, these gifts have been manifested through Christians who are baptized with the Holy Spirit as evidenced by their ability to speak (praise and glorify God) in another language (tongue) unlearned by them (Acts 2:4, 8, 11; 10:45, 46).

The supernatural gifts for service are given according to the character of the ministry that is to be performed. The power and purpose of God is evidenced through the Holy Spirit as people minister. The Holy Spirit confirms their ministry with signs of God's power (Mark 16:20; 1 Corinthians 12:7-11).

GIFTS OF THE SPIRIT

Who "Works" the Manifestations

Except for Jesus commissioning the 70 and the 12 (Matthew 10; Luke 10), it was only after the Holy Spirit was poured out upon the first disciples that the supernatural gifts began working through them. Therefore, only after you have become a child of God and have received the baptism with the Holy Spirit, are you eligible to minister the supernatural gifts. It is apparent that the ministry resulting from supernatural gifts confirms the message of the gospel (Mark 16:17, 18, 20).

A Christian is encouraged to abound in the things of the Lord, but to seek first the Kingdom of God (Matthew 6:33). The King of God's Kingdom is Jesus. Direct your attention to Him and worship Him as the Giver of the gift of the Holy Spirit. Avoid the tendency to regard the gifts as measures of spirituality. You are known by your fruit, not your gifts. The fruit (virtues or God's qualities) of the Spirit are available to all Christians (Galatians 5:22, 23). All Christians can bear fruit (good works). Gifts are given differently for the good of all.

You should seek out fellowship with other Christians whose faith has been increased because of the gifts of the Holy Spirit. You may already be attending a Spirit-filled church where the gifts are being manifested. If you need help in understanding the baptism with the Holy Spirit or the gifts of the Holy Spirit, seek a Spirit-filled pastor or counselor who will help you.

As You Pray

Pray in faith. Receive Jesus, the Giver of the Holy Spirit. Allow Him to fill you with His Spirit. Recognize that you are now able to freely receive His gifts as directed by the Holy Spirit. Pray for the greatest gift—love. Pray that you will recognize when God is putting you in a place of service for the use of His gifts.

References/Homework

Read *Gifts of the Spirit,* Gordon Lindsay; *The Gifts of the Spirit,* Harold Horton; *The Dynamics of Spiritual Gifts,* William McRae; and *19 Gifts of the Spirit,* Leslie B. Flynn.

GIFTS OF THE SPIRIT

John 14	The Holy Spirit promised
John 15	Jesus, the source for bearing fruit
John 16	The work of the Holy Spirit
1 Corinthians 13	The excellence of love in ministering gifts
Acts 7:54-60; 12:1-5	Gift of martyrdom: Stephen's and James' martyrdom
1 Corinthians 7:7, 8	Gift of celibacy: Paul

Notes

_____

_____

_____

_____

_____

_____

_____

_____

_____

GIVING AND TITHING

To give is a spiritual principle of the Kingdom of God and is a part of the law of reciprocity: as you give, it will be given unto you. The Bible in both the Old and New Testaments speaks of the stewardship or management of our material wealth. This can include the tithing and giving of money or objects of value in lieu of money. We are responsible for that which we have received and we are to freely give of it.

Tithes and offerings are examples of giving. To tithe is to present a tenth of your prosperity to God. An offering is given after you have given the tithe. Also, the poor or otherwise needy are to be recipients of our giving (Deuteronomy 15:11; Proverbs 3:9, 10).

What Scripture Says

"Will a man rob God? Yet ye have robbed me. But ye say, Wherein have we robbed thee? In tithes and offerings. Ye are cursed with a curse: for ye have robbed me, even this whole nation. Bring ye all the tithes into the storehouse, that there may be meat in mine house, and prove me now herewith, saith the Lord of hosts, if I will not open you the windows of heaven, and pour you out a blessing, that there shall not be room enough to receive it. And I will rebuke the devourer for your sakes, and he shall not destroy the fruits of your ground; neither shall your vine cast her fruit before the time in the field, saith the Lord of hosts" (Malachi 3:8-11).

"Take heed that ye do not your alms before men, to be seen of them: otherwise ye have no reward of your Father which is in heaven" (Matthew 6:1).

"Give, and it shall be given unto you; good measure, pressed down, and shaken together, and running over, shall men give into your bosom. For with the same measure that ye mete withal it shall be measured to you again" (Luke 6:38).

GIVING AND TITHING

"But this I say, He which soweth sparingly shall reap also sparingly; and he which soweth bountifully shall reap also bountifully. Every man *according as he purposeth in his heart,* so let him give; not grudgingly, or of necessity: for God loveth a cheerful giver. And God is able to make all grace abound toward you; that ye, always having all sufficiency in all things, may abound to every good work: (As it is written, He hath dispersed abroad; he hath given to the poor: his righteousness remaineth for ever. Now he that ministereth seed to the sower both minister bread for your food, and multiply your seed sown, and increase the fruits of your righteousness); Being enriched in every thing to all bountifulness, which causeth through us thanksgiving to God. For the administration of this service not only supplieth the want of the saints, but is abundant also by many thanksgivings unto God" (2 Corinthians 9:6-12).

"He that hath pity upon the poor lendeth unto the Lord; and that which he hath given will he pay him again" (Proverbs 19:17).

As You Give

In the Old Testament, the Jews were required to tithe by law. One tenth of the wealth God had given them was to be returned to God's work. In the New Testament, Christians are obligated to tithe and give offerings under God's grace. If you are wondering whether to practice tithing and giving, study the Scriptures cited above. Try tithing for six months. If you are to be convinced of the importance of tithing, the Holy Spirit will have convinced you by then. The tithe and offering should be given as the Holy Spirit impresses you to give.

Remember than an offering is given after the tithe. Giving is not an offering until the requirement of the tithe is first met. Giving should be done willingly, no matter what the amount.

The Bible says that tithes are to be brought to the storehouse. The local congregation that ministers to you is commonly understood to be that storehouse (Malachi 3:8-11). If you have no particular local congregation with which you are identified, look for a Bible-believing church with Spirit-filled ministers and teachers.

You may also wish to give to the Church in a broader sense. There are many avenues of giving. Other ministries can be given to through your local congregation or directly. Normally, they should be given to after tithing to your local congregation.

You must decide how to account for your stewardship of tithes and offerings as the Spirit leads. God promises that as you honor Him with your tithes, offerings and gifts, you will receive again as you have given. May God bless you as you are obedient in your stewardship to Him.

As You Pray

Offer a prayer of commitment to tithe and give offerings. In faith, commit yourself to trust God's Word. Determine that your motives shall be simply to honor God in your giving.

References/Homework

Matthew 22:15-22	Render to Caesar his own
Luke 6:38	Give and receive good measure
1 Corinthians 16:1, 2	Giving to needy saints

Notes

_____

_____

_____

_____

_____

_____

_____

_____

_____

_____

GOSSIP

Gossip is sharing private information with those who are not part of the problem or part of the solution.

When you speak things about others that you would be ashamed to say in their presence, you are not only disobeying God's Word (Leviticus 19:16), you are also destroying that person's reputation in the mind of your listener. Scripture states that the sin of gossip is not limited to the spreading of lies alone, but also to the improper involvement of yourself in another's personal business (1 Timothy 5:13). Even to participate in the act of gossip as a listener is sin (Proverbs 20:19, NASB). In willfully listening to the one who gossips, you sanction his destruction of the other person's reputation.

What Scripture Says

"For I fear, lest, when I come, I shall not find you as I would, and that I shall be found unto you such as ye would not: lest there be debates, envyings, wraths, strifes, backbitings, whisperings, swellings, tumults" (2 Corinthians 12:20).

"Thou shalt not go up and down as a talebearer among thy people: neither shalt thou stand against the blood of thy neighbour: I am the Lord" (Leviticus 19:16).

"And withal they learn to be idle, wandering about from house to house; and not only idle, but tattlers also and busybodies, speaking things which they ought not" (1 Timothy 5:13).

"For I heard the defaming of many, fear on every side. Report, say they, and we will report it. All my familiars watched for my halting, . . . we shall take our revenge on him" (Jeremiah 20:10).

"And the soldiers likewise demanded of him, saying, And what shall we do? And he said unto them, Do violence to no man, neither accuse any falsely; and be content with your wages" (Luke 3:14).

"Speak no evil one of another, brethren. He that speaketh evil of his brother, and judgeth his brother, speaketh evil of the law, and judgeth the law: but if thou judge the law, thou art not a doer of the law, but a judge. There is no lawgiver, who is able to save and to destroy: who art thou that judgest another?" (James 4:11, 12).

"Moreover, if thy brother shall trespass against thee, go and tell him his fault between thee and him alone . . ." (Matthew 18:15).

God's Alternative

Matthew 18:15 gives the scriptural alternative to gossip. If you have something against someone, you should go to that person, tell him your grievance, and hear his side of the story. It may be that you were wrong. Thus, you will not only clear up your misunderstanding, but you will have a chance to apologize as well.

On the other hand, if you were correct and the person's words or actions have in some way caused you or another harm, then that person is given the opportunity to repent and "thou hast gained thy brother." Scripture gives further instruction concerning the course to take if the brother does not repent (Matthew 18:16, 17).

When you find yourself gossiping, repent at once so that God will forgive you of this terrible, destructive sin. Gossip has its roots in jealousy, hate and self-pride. As with hate, you remove the person who is the object of your gossip from the love you should be showing him (1 John 2:9, 11; 3:15). As a result, you murder him in your heart.

In order to overcome gossiping, seek the fruit of the Spirit: love, joy, peace, patience, kindness, goodness, faithfulness, gentleness and self-control. As you acquire these virtues, you will not be boastfully challenging and envying other persons (Galatians 5:22-26). Instead, you will find yourself able to think of others as worthy of your love and respect. As you then show love, honor and respect, you will receive love, honor and respect.

As You Pray

Pray in this way:

Please forgive me Lord, for being a part of gossip, both for listening to it and for passing it on. Let the words of my mouth and the meditation of my heart be acceptable in your sight. In Jesus' name, Amen.

References/Homework

Read *Beauty Care for the Tongue,* LeRoy Koapman; *The Christian Counselor's Manual,* Jay Adams, pp. 58, 59.

1 Corinthians 13:1ff.	Love does not seek its own
Romans 1:29	Whispering
Romans 1:30	Backbiting
1 Timothy 6:4	Evil surmising
Ecclesiastes 10:1	Babbling
Psalm 41:5	Evil speaking
Exodus 20:16	Bearing false witness
Proverbs 17:9	Reporting matters

Notes

_____

_____

_____

_____

_____

_____

_____

_____

_____

GRIEF/DEATH

A deep hurt because of the loss of a loved one can cause feelings of depression, sorrow, pain, emptiness and loneliness that take longer than you would like to overcome.

It is the lot of man to grieve over the loss of loved ones. For the Christian, the hope we have in Jesus carries us through any such time of sorrow or pain (1 Thessalonians 4:13).

What Scripture Says

"Let not your heart be troubled: ye believe in God, believe also in me. In my Father's house are many mansions: if it were not so, I would have told you. I go to prepare a place for you. And if I go and prepare a place for you, I will come again, and receive you unto myself; that where I am, there ye may be also" (Christians' hope) (John 14:1-3).

"For now we see through a glass, darkly; but then face to face: now I know in part; but then shall I know even as also I am known" (Understanding promised) (1 Corinthians 13:12).

"Jesus said unto her, I am the resurrection, and the life: he that believeth in me, though he were dead, yet shall he live" (John 11:25).

"For me to live is Christ, and to die is gain" (No fear in Christ) (Philippians 1:21).

"Blessed are they that mourn: for they shall be comforted" (Matthew 5:4).

For You Personally

Seek the Lord in silent prayer and praise. He is always near you, only a prayer away.

If the deceased loved one was a Christian, allow the Scriptures cited above to comfort you. May the comfort and hope, peace and assurance of God's love and concern be yours in your grief.

GRIEF/DEATH

If you are not a Christian, please receive this word to you, knowing that it is given in love. It is for us who are now alive to prepare ourselves to meet God. God's word to you if you are not already prepared is one of assurance that you can be. The one who is now dead had already made whatever preparation he or she could make. If you are not sure that you have done so, follow this simple plan of salvation. Call on the Lord to forgive you and save you from your sins. Give yourself to Him with the simple faith that He will come into your life as you do. Receive Him as both your Savior and Lord of your life. As you do, He will forgive you, cleanse you and cause you to be known as a child of God (John 1:12; Romans 10:10, 13; 1 John 1:8, 9).

If the deceased person was a child, you should know the story of Jeroboam's son who became sick. God said He was taking the child because He saw a good thing in the child (1 Kings 14:1, 13).

Also David's experience of losing a son is a word for you. His hope was in God and he prayed that the child would live. The child died, but David knew he must go on with the business of living. He could go to the child, but the child could not return to him (2 Samuel 12:22, 23).

There is hope in the stories of Jeroboam's and David's sons because they show that, often, God sees into the future and allows the child to die, sparing some later tragedy. These passages indicate that God may take a child (or Christian adult) to be with Him in heaven. You can prepare yourself to be with that child or adult who has died.

In the Bible (Matthew 5:4; 2 Corinthians 1:3-5), Jesus promised comfort for everyone who mourns. It is one of the missions of the Holy Spirit to give peace to your heart (Galatians 5:22). You are assured of perfect peace as you turn your heart toward God and trust Him (Isaiah 26:3). Let your mind dwell on the Lord by offering thanksgiving and praise to Him, especially in this time of grief. He works it for good to those who love Him and are called by Him (Romans 8:28).

Your pastor is there to pray with you and to share God's Word with you in this time of need. If you do not have a church at this time, look for a Bible-believing church near you.

As You Pray

Pray and thank God for His peace and assurance to you. Allow His love and grace to fill your heart during these hours. May God's peace, comfort and blessing be yours as you pray.

References/Homework

1 Corinthians 15	The resurrection of the dead
Psalm 23	The Lord our Shepherd
2 Corinthians 5:1-9	Our house in heaven
1 Peter 1:3-5	Eternal inheritance
Philippians 1:21	To die is gain
Psalm 30:5	Joy promised again

Notes

_____

_____

_____

_____

_____

_____

_____

_____

GUIDANCE

If you are seeking God's will regarding a certain aspect of your life, or searching for His leading in a decision you face, be assured that God has a plan for all matters. If you seek Him first before making your plans, instead of leaning on your own understanding, He will meet all your needs and direct your path.

What Scripture Says

"Woe to the rebellious children, saith the Lord, that take counsel, but not of me; and that cover with a covering, but not of my spirit, that they may add sin to sin" (Isaiah 30:1).

"But seek ye first the kingdom of God, and his righteousness: and all these things shall be added unto you" (Matthew 6:33).

"Trust in the Lord with all thine heart; and lean not unto thine own understanding. In all thy ways acknowledge him, and he shall direct thy paths" (Proverbs 3:5, 6).

"All the ways of a man are clean in his own eyes; but the Lord weigheth the spirits. Commit thy works unto the Lord, and thy thoughts shall be established" (Proverbs 16:2, 3).

"Every way of a man is right in his own eyes: but the Lord pondereth the hearts" (Proverbs 21:2).

"The meek [submissive] will he guide in judgment" (Psalm 25:9a).

"Howbeit when he, the Spirit of truth, is come, he will guide you into all truth: for he shall not speak of himself; but whatsoever he shall hear, that he shall speak: and he will shew you things to come" (John 16:13).

"But the wisdom that is from above is first pure, then peaceable, gentle, and easy to be entreated, full of mercy and good fruits, without partiality, and without hypocrisy" (James 3:17).

Preparation for Guidance

Sometimes God speaks to people even though they do not realize it is He. However, to know the voice of God, you need to be a born-again Christian. The natural man cannot receive the things of the Spirit of God, neither can he know them. They are spiritually discerned (1 Corinthians 2:14). Ask God to baptize you with His Holy Spirit which will give you greater discernment.

God's Word must always be your authority and first source of guidance. The Bible clearly states whether or not many attitudes, thoughts and actions are in accordance with God's will. Any decision or course of action that would be in disagreement with what the Bible teaches is wrong.

If your decision or plan of action agrees with God's Word, look for God to confirm His will for you through one or two other sources such as the Holy Spirit or circumstances. According to Scripture, a thing is established when there are two or more witnesses. This usually means that the Bible and circumstances agree with a course of action and the Spirit bears witness with peace.

If God Is Saying "No"

Expect the Holy Spirit to make you feel uneasy or uncertain in your heart if you shouldn't do something. You may feel somewhat fearful about a particular course of action or inaction (Proverbs 16:2; 21:2).

Expect God to close or open doors to opportunities as you acknowledge Him. Don't be angry if He shuts a door you wanted open (Proverbs 3:5, 6). God is not the author of confusion. If you are experiencing confusion, change or reevaluate your decision.

As You Pray

Thank and praise God for revealing His will to you. As you do so, expect Him to reveal something that will help you in making a correct decision. Expect verification. Look for confirmation of God's will. This may include a word from God from another source, circumstances that bring to pass what was revealed or Scriptures that confirm God's message.

GUIDANCE

References/Homework
Read *Guidance Guidelines,* Katie Fortune, Aglow Publications, 7715 236th SW, Edmonds, WA 98020.

Psalm 73:24	God's counsel
Isaiah 30:21	Ears will hear
Isaiah 42:16	Expect unknown paths
Proverbs 16:1	God will prepare your heart and give answers for the tongue
Proverbs 16:3	Commit works to the Lord—thoughts established
Proverbs 3:5, 6	God will direct your path
Proverbs 21:1	God turns hearts of men
Proverbs 21:2	Heart is pondered
John 14:26	God's Word brought to remembrance
John 16:12-15	Jesus will reveal His desire through the Spirit

Notes

_____

_____

_____

_____

_____

_____

_____

_____

_____

GUILT

You may feel guilty because of something you said, thought or did that was wrong and against God's commandments. If so, the Holy Spirit is speaking to your spirit, telling you that you have sinned. Or maybe someone said something that makes you feel guilty. Or perhaps you are blaming yourself for something bad for which you feel responsible.

Guilt is God's way of warning us to repent and turn away from our sins so He can forgive us, cleanse us and make us entirely guilt-free. If you are guilty, you have broken the law and you deserve punishment. However, you can receive mercy and forgiveness by accepting the salvation and forgiveness offered through our Lord Jesus Christ (1 Timothy 1:13-16).

What Scripture Says

"Bless the Lord . . . Who forgiveth all thine iniquities; who healeth all thy diseases" (Psalm 103:2, 3).

"For if ye forgive men their trespasses, your heavenly Father will also forgive you" (Matthew 6:14).

"In whom we have redemption through his blood, the forgiveness of sins, according to the riches of his grace. . . . For by grace are ye saved through faith; and that not of yourselves: it is the gift of God: Not of works, lest any man should boast" (Ephesians 1:7; 2:8, 9).

"For the wages of sin is death; but the gift of God is eternal life through Jesus Christ our Lord. . . . That if thou shalt confess with thy mouth the Lord Jesus, and shalt believe in thine heart that God hath raised him from the dead, thou shalt be saved. For with the heart man believeth unto righteousness; and with the mouth confession is made unto salvation" (Romans 6:23; 10:9, 10).

"If we confess our sins, he is faithful and just to forgive us our

GUILT

sins, and to cleanse us from all unrighteousness" (1 John 1:9).

"Therefore if any man be in Christ, he is a new creature: old things are passed away: behold, all things are become new" (2 Corinthians 5:17).

What to Do with Guilt

Have you been saved? Do you have assurance of your salvation or are you trying to work it out or do penance for it? Have you forgiven yourself after asking God to forgive you?

Someone may have said or done something that makes you feel guilty whether you are at fault or not. In either case, it is important to repent of any wrongdoing for which you are clearly guilty. Make restitution for any wrongs if at all possible. Do not harbor unforgiveness or do anything that will bring more guilt. When you have repented, God will remove any guilt from your sins. There is freedom from condemnation when you are in Christ (Romans 8:1).

If someone has tried to make you feel guilty and it is undeserved, don't harbor hurt feelings or unforgiveness in your heart. Don't seek vengeance or do anything for which you should feel guilty. Instead, ask God to forgive anyone who wrongfully accuses you. Ask Him to help you love that person. Tell the person you feel wrongfully accused, but that you forgive him and have asked God to help you love him. Ask God to help the two of you resolve the conflict.

God wants to free you from anything that would hinder your full life and liberty in Him. Christ has taken your guilt upon Himself. You are free from guilt the very moment you believe in your heart and confess it with your mouth.

As You Pray

Ask the Lord Jesus Christ to completely forgive you for every sin you have ever committed. Receive Christ's joy in your life. As you thank and praise Him, release the burden of guilt to God. Be sure to intercede for anyone else who may have been involved in the situation for which you were burdened.

References/Homework

1 John 1:7-9	God's light dispels darkness and fellowship is promised
John 1:12; 5:24; 8:36	Belief in Christ delivers from sin
Romans 6:18, 22; 8:1	Freedom from sin and guilt
Colossians 2:13-22	Assurance of salvation
Psalm 103:12	Our sins completely separated from us
Isaiah 1:18	Sins are cleansed
Jeremiah 31:34	No remembrance of sin by God (cf. Hebrews 8:12)
Philippians 3:13, 14	The prize of God's high calling

Notes

_____

_____

_____

_____

_____

_____

_____

_____

HEALING

When you are experiencing illness, disease, infirmity or other physical, mental or spiritual problems, you should seek God for healing.

God wants you to be whole. He is sovereign and desires to make His children vessels fit for good works. He wants you healed and whole *until* He takes away your breath at His appointed time (Psalm 104:29). In fact, Jesus bore your stripes in His own body so that you might be healed.

What Scripture Says

"Surely he hath borne our griefs, and carried our sorrows: yet we did esteem him stricken, smitten of God, and afflicted. But he was wounded for our transgressions, he was bruised for our iniquities; the chastisement of our peace was upon him; and with his stripes we *are healed*" (Isaiah 53:4, 5).

"For he hath made him to be sin for us, who knew no sin; that we might be made the righteousness of God in him" (2 Corinthians 5:21). (God declares the born-again person to be righteous in Christ.)

"Again I say unto you, that if two of you shall *agree* on earth as touching any thing that they shall ask, *it shall be done* for them of my Father which is in heaven" (Matthew 18:19).

"Therefore I say unto you, What things soever ye desire, when ye pray, *believe* that ye receive them, and ye shall have them" (Mark 11:24).

"For with the heart man *believeth* unto righteousness; and with the mouth *confession* is made unto salvation" (Romans 10:10). (Your salvation includes your health.)

"And this is the confidence that we have in him, that, if we ask any thing according to his will, he heareth us: And if we *know that he hears us,* whatsover we ask, we *know that we have the petitions* that we desired of him" (1 John 5:14, 15). (He desires that we be saved, whole, healed.)

Steps to Healing

Your spiritual health is determined by your relationship with Christ, and God's offer of salvation to you includes your physical health.

You may wish to ask someone to pray with you. Agree together in prayer that God is going to answer. Stand on God's Word rather than trust in symptoms (James 1:6-8).

1. Believe and confess salvation (Romans 10:9-13; 1 John 1:8, 9).
2 Agree with each other (Matthew 18:19).
3 Take God at His Word (Isaiah 53:4, 5).
4. Receive your healing by faith (Mark 11:24).
5. Continue in the Lord, leaning and growing (Exodus 15:26).

If Symptoms Persist

If symptoms of a problem remain, they may indicate that there are *barriers* God wants removed before He completes the healing. Barriers may include:

1. Harboring iniquity in the heart (Psalm 66:18). If our hearts don't condemn us we have confidence that God will answer our prayers (1 John 3:21).

2. Need to renounce cult or occult activity and false religious teachings (Deuteronomy 18:10-13).

3. Doubt, fear, anxiety, worry, unforgiveness, bitterness and other barriers to faith (James 4:7; Ephesians 6:11, 12).

4. Not having a wholehearted desire to be healed. For example, illness may be like a security blanket or "old friend" you don't really want to lose.

5. Stopping short of total healing after one problem or symptom is gone, but before the goal of total wholeness is reached.

6. God may be doing a parallel work in another person or situation, such as your spouse, relative, etc. If so, He may be bringing it all together, one thing bearing on the other. Begin praising God for the healing which will be manifested at a later date.

7. Need to be delivered from spiritual bondage.

There may be time when you will feel "checked" from praying for healing (Proverbs 16:2) or lose faith that God will heal. If so, you can still ask God to work on your behalf. Don't limit Him. Commit yourself into His hands. Bind Satan in Jesus' name and praise God in His mercy and sovereignty. Pray, expecting God to bless in His love.

Seek out a Spirit-filled fellowship if you are not already part of one. We all need the growth and edification that fellowship brings. It will help you learn how to maintain your spiritual status and go from victory to victory.

CAUTION: A counselor or prayer partner should not advise you to cease taking medicine or medical treatment. If you believe God wants you to stop taking a medicine or treatment, do so in agreement with your doctor. A counselor cannot act as an expert in such matters.

As You Pray

The prayer of thanksgiving and praise is acceptable to God. He answers before we ask. We can praise Him for His grace and love to us and for answering our prayers to heal. Remember that healing is sometimes a process, although a miracle of healing may be instantaneous.

Reference/Homework.

Read *Healing the Sick and Casting Out Demons,* T.L. Osborne.

Romans 10:17; John 8:31-32	Faith
Deuteronomy 28:15-62; Galatians 3:13	Redeemed from the law's curse
John 15:7	Abide in Christ
Philippians 4:13-19	A good confession
2 Timothy 1:7	A good confession
1 Peter 2:24, 25	A good confession
Matthew 10:32, 33	A good confession
John 14:12; James 4:7	Going on
2 Corinthians 12:7-10	Beware of Satan's messenger

Job 3:25   Fear
Hebrews 10:35, 36;   Observe these
     Mark 11:24
Proverbs 4:20-22;   Observe these
     Exodus 15:26

Notes

_____

_____

_____

_____

_____

_____

_____

_____

HOLY SPIRIT BAPTISM

As a Christian, there is something more for you once you are born again by the Spirit of God. You can be baptized with the Holy Spirit. If this aspect of your relationship with God is lacking, you will always thirst in your heart for fulfillment.

The baptism with the Holy Spirit is the overflowing of the Holy Spirit into, upon and out of a born-again believer. It is the fulfillment of the promise the Father gave to all believers. It leads to a full, purposeful, meaningful and rewarding life in Jesus Christ (Joel 2:28, 29; Acts 2:16-18).

Upon receiving the baptism with the Holy Spirit, you are also eligible to receive all the blessings and gifts of the Holy Spirit (Galatians 5:22, 23; 1 Corinthians 12:1-7). It is the Holy Spirit who empowers you to be a witness for Christ with signs following (Mark 16:20; John 14:12; 16:8, 13-15).

What Scripture Says

"For John truly baptized with water; but ye shall be baptized with the Holy Ghost not many days hence" (Acts 1:5).

"But ye shall receive power, after that the Holy Ghost is come upon you: and ye shall be witnesses unto me both in Jerusalem, and in all Judaea, and in Samaria, and unto the uttermost part of the earth" (Acts 1:8).

"And they were all filled with the Holy Ghost, and began to speak with other tongues, as the Spirit gave them utterance" (Acts 2:4).

"But this is that which was spoken by the prophet Joel; And it shall come to pass in the last days, saith God, I will pour out of my Spirit upon all flesh: and your sons and your daughters shall prophesy, and your young men shall see visions, and your old men shall dream dreams" (Acts 2:16, 17).

"For the promise is unto you, and to your children, and to all that are afar off, even as many as the Lord our God shall call" (Acts 2:39).

"If ye then, being evil, know how to give good gifts unto your children: how much more shall your heavenly Father give the Holy Spirit to them that ask him?" (Luke 11:13).

How to Receive

The baptism with the Holy Spirit is only for a born-again child of God. Therefore, you must first repent of sin. Renounce the occult, fortune-telling, and horoscopes, if you have been involved with them. Forgive any who have wronged you. Then call upon the Lord to save and forgive you and to make you a child of God (Romans 10:13; 1 John 1:9; John 1:12).

In Luke 11:13, Jesus says the Father will give you the Holy Spirit if you ask Him. By faith, take Jesus at His word. He is the one who baptizes with the Holy Spirit. Agree with Him that you are being baptized with the Holy Spirit once you have asked to be.

Upon receiving the Holy Spirit, you should be able to speak in a language you have not learned. Speaking in an unlearned language is the evidence which accompanies the baptism with the Holy Spirit. It has occurred since the day of Pentecost and was a prime evidence of the Holy Spirit baptism experienced by the early Christians (Acts 2:4; 10:46; 19:6).

Once you have asked for the baptism, ask God to anoint you. Then in quiet praise and worship, wait for the anointing, the witness and the evidence to come forth. Expect it! Rejoice in it!

Open your heart to receive the Holy Spirit. Your spirit is crying out to God. What is happening is spirit-to-Spirit communication with God.

Relax in the Lord, and as you focus your attention on Him, give your heart and tongue to Him in praise and adoration. Remember that the Holy Spirit will give the utterance. However, it is you who will cause the sounds to come forth. It is through your speech faculties—tongue, mouth, breath, etc.—that the Spirit speaks.

If, after a period of time, you discern that the evidence of a Spirit-given language is not forthcoming, do not despair. God will give the evidence. You are a unique individual, and your experience will be your own. But believe that God is faithful. Continue to wait before Him in praise. Offer any sound, syllable, word or phrase you don't understand as praise to God. You may even begin to sing in the Spirit-given language.

When you receive your language, it may seem like babbling baby talk, or it may be a melodic, inspiring utterance. Accept it as from the Spirit and give glory to God. You are the final judge of whether your language or communication is of the Spirit. "Test the spirits." You have asked God and you are giving Him glory and honoring Him in praise, so you can know that He will honor you in return. He will not withhold any good thing from His children. He will give you what you ask (John 14:13; Luke 11:13).

One of the principles of the Kingdom of God concerns being in agreement with Him and with another as you pray. Be encouraged to ask another Spirit-filled Christian, such as a pastor or friend, to pray with you.

It is possible that you have asked to receive the baptism with the Holy Spirit before in your life. Perhaps you spoke in what you thought was "made-up gibberish." But God is faithful and will not give you something unintelligible to Him regardless of how it sounds to you. Continue to offer praise to God and pray in that language. Offer it to God as a praise to Him, and even sacrifice praise in it. Fluency in a language comes with usage.

As You Pray

Offer thanksgiving and praise to God for baptizing you with the Spirit. As you are praising God, thank Him for meeting further needs, such as healing for your family or relatives. Praise Him for His blessings. Praise Him for all things and in all things (Ephesians 5:20; 1 Thessalonians 5:18).

References/Homework

Joel 2:28, 29	Prophecy
Acts 2:16-18	Prophecy
John 14, 16	Promised by Jesus

HOLY SPIRIT BAPTISM

Acts 1:5-8	Promised by Jesus
Acts 2	Fulfillment
Acts 2:1-11	Evidence
Acts 10:44-48	At salvation
Acts 19:1-7	After salvation
1 Corinthians 14:4	Tongues of edification
Isaiah 28:11, 12	For rest in the Lord

Worship with a Spirit-filled body of believers and begin to grow in understanding, experience, wisdom and knowledge. As you experience a greater faith and joy in the Lord, you will also find yourself experiencing more of a fullness and spiritual growth. When you speak with another tongue (language not learned) you edify yourself (1 Corinthians 14:4). You are being "built up" in the Spirit.

Notes

_____

_____

_____

_____

_____

_____

_____

_____

HOMOSEXUALITY

Homosexuality is a deviant relationship where two people of the same sex lust after each other or engage in a sexual relationship. Homosexuals are often referred to as being "gay." Homosexuality is a behavioral sin that creates tremendous emotional and social problems.

The Word of God calls homosexuality an abomination. It is in rebellion to God's original plan for humankind. He intended for one man and one woman to be united together for life, and that they be fruitful and multiply, thus establishing the home and the priesthood in the home (Leviticus 18:22; 20:13). Homosexuality is far less than the best God has for you.

What Scripture Says

"If a man also lie with mankind, as he lieth with a woman, both of them have committed an abomination: they shall surely be put to death; their blood shall be upon them" (Leviticus 20:13).

"Know ye not that the unrighteous shall not inherit the kingdom of God? Be not deceived: neither fornicators, nor idolaters, nor adulterers, nor effeminate, nor abusers of themselves with mankind [homosexuals] . . ." (1 Corinthians 6:9).

"For whoremongers, for them that defile themselves with mankind [homosexuals], for menstealers, for liars, for perjured persons, and if there be any other thing that is contrary to sound doctrine" (The law was made for such) (1 Timothy 1:10).

"Because that, when they knew God, they glorified him not as God, neither were thankful; but became vain in their imaginations, and their foolish heart was darkened . . . women did change the natural use into that which is against nature: . . . men . . . burned in their lust one toward another; . . . they that commit such things are worthy of death . . ." (Romans 1:21, 26, 27, 32).

132

"Likewise reckon ye also yourselves to be dead indeed unto sin, but alive unto God through Jesus Christ our Lord. *Let not sin therefore reign* in your mortal body, that ye should obey it in the lusts thereof. Neither yield ye your members as instruments of unrighteousness unto sin: but *yield* yourselves *unto God,* as those that are alive from the dead, and your members as instruments of righteousness unto God. For sin shall not have dominion over you: for ye are not under the law, but under grace. . . . But now being made free from sin, and become servants to God, ye have your fruit unto holiness, and the end everlasting life" (Romans 6:11-14, 22).

How to Be Free from This Curse

No matter how you came to be under the curse of this sin, you can be free from it. Its end is physical, mental, and spiritual destruction. Do not be deceived. It is a mockery to God and you will reap what you sow in this sin (Galatians 6:7). Take a bold, fearless inventory of your life. Determine to make it count for righteousness.

To be free, you must start with the right relationship with God. You must be born again of the Spirit of God. Do you want to be a child of God? Repent of all your sins. God loves you. He will forgive you, save you and include you among all His redeemed (Romans 10:13; 1 John 1:8, 9; John 1:12).

If you are already born again, have you been baptized with the Holy Spirit? You need the ability to know the difference between sin and righteousness and to be able to do something about sin. The Holy Spirit provides that ability.

You are eligible to receive the baptism with the Holy Spirit (John 14:16; Luke 11:13; Acts 1:8) after you have been born again of the Spirit of God (John 3). Ask Jesus to fill you with the Holy Spirit. In faith, receive the Holy Spirit into your heart. If you need further assistance and explanation, other Spirit-filled Christians will be happy to help you and pray with you.

In 2 Timothy 3:3 we are warned that in the last days men shall be "without natural affections." Unless you are under the conviction of the Holy Spirit and repent, you will inevitably be angry and defensive about your lifestyle. Please accept this counsel as being given out of God's love for you. It is impossible to glorify God unless you forsake your sin. Forsake your past lifestyle and begin to move into relationships involving Christ and His Church. Abstain from further association with those involved in homosexual activity.

Remember: the alternative to homosexuality is not heterosexuality. It is dealing with the lust that creates or heightens the desire to sin. Even if you have turned to God and then fallen back into sin before, be encouraged to again repent of your backsliding and go on with Christ. He does not condemn you. He loves you (John 3:16; Jeremiah 2:19; Isaiah 55:7). Also, read 1 Thessalonians 5:14b; Galatians 6:1; 1 John 1:9.

How to Stay Free

As with other deviant behavior, there is a pattern of circumstances which leads to the homosexual act. When the pattern is known, deliberately engaging in a different behavioral pattern can lead away from the desire and the act. To recognize the pattern, start at the act or the desire to act, and trace actions, thoughts and routines backward to the place you can recognize as the beginning of the pattern. The beginning of the pattern needs to be recognized. Often you will realize that the same or similar circumstance has been the beginning each time you went on to do the act. At its beginning is the best place to change the pattern. Deliberately do something different.

An acceptable and victorious alternative is in acts of praise and worship of God. Learn the principle of praising God. He will minister to you to deliver you from this problem. Also, the Church's ministry is designed by God to help a person know God in all His fullness. Attend a Bible-believing, no-compromise, Spirit-filled church. (Caution: Don't be deceived by so-called "gay churches.")

Look for new role models. Work and worship with heterosexual Christians who really care about you. At this point in your life, you may only relate the affections of someone of the same sex to "the act of sex." You need instead to be around people who love you without sexual connotations. Get involved in a Christian fellowship where you can learn disciplined living (Romans 6:7-23).

134

It is important for your mind to be renewed. Rather than being "conformed to this world, be ye transformed by the renewing of your mind" (Romans 12:2). Receive the fruit of the Spirit—love, joy, peace, patience, kindness, goodness, faithfulness, humility, and self-control (Galatians 5:22, 23). These are God's own character traits or virtues. The Holy Spirit will produce them within you and they will replace the worldly, fleshly nature which resulted in the homosexuality.

Another need is to acquire and walk in God's armor: truth, righteousness, the Gospel, faith, salvation and a good knowledge of the Bible. With His armor, you will be able to stand against the deceit and temptations of Satan (Ephesians 6:10-18). God's armor comes from knowing and doing God's Word. It is necessary for victorious living.

"Saturate" yourself with Scripture. It is important to "feast" your mind on the wholesomeness of God's Word. What you think is determined by what you read, watch, hear or are otherwise exposed to. What you think about determines what you become and are. To resist temptation, have your mind stayed on God rather than temptation or sin. Praise and thanksgiving offered to God continuously will assure peace from temptations (Isaiah 26:3; Ephesians 5:20; 1 Thessalonians 5:18; Hebrews 13:15; Psalm 22:3).

Old thoughts and actions (habit patterns) that lead you to the homosexual acts should be discovered and changed. To do this, you may need the help of a Bible-believing church and perhaps the special counsel and ministry of a Christian counselor. Do not hesitate to seek help. It's your life, your soul. It's too important to you, to God, to your family and to other people for you to wait or leave things to chance. Take definite steps to change. You will find that God has provided an abundant (full, meaningful, purposeful) life for you in Christ Jesus (John 10:10).

As You Pray

Pray in the power of the Spirit and the authority of Jesus, renouncing lust and homosexual desire. Thank and praise God continually for freedom from lust and the spirit of homosexuality, for victory and newness of life in Christ and for the overcoming power of the Holy Spirit.

References/Homework

Genesis 19	The result of homosexuality
Romans 1	The result of rebellion against God
Galatians 5	Fleshly behavior versus God's nature

Notes

_____

_____

_____

_____

_____

_____

_____

_____

HOPE

If you are seeking hope in some difficult circumstances, but are experiencing anguish, despair and hopelessness, be encouraged in the Lord. God is the ultimate source for eternal hope. The Bible was written with the purpose of meeting your need (Romans 15:14).

What Scripture Says

"For we are saved by hope: but hope that is seen is not hope: for what a man seeth, why doth he yet hope for?" (Romans 8:24).

"To him give all the prophets witness, that through his name whosoever believeth in him shall receive remission of sins" (Acts 10:43).

"Peace I leave with you, my peace I give unto you: not as the world giveth, give I unto you. Let not your heart be troubled, neither let it be afraid" (John 14:27).

"That which we have seen and heard declare we unto you, that ye also may have fellowship with us: and truly our fellowship is with the Father, and with his Son Jesus Christ" (1 John 1:3).

"Come unto me, all ye that labour and are heavy laden, and I will give you rest. Take my yoke upon you, and learn of me; for I am meek and lowly in heart: and ye shall find rest unto your souls. For my yoke is easy, and my burden is light" (Matthew 11:28-30).

Hope for You

God has made the above and additional promises to those who believe in Him. Every promise in the Bible, God says, is "yea and amen" in Christ. You have favor with God. He will see to it that you have favor with men. You need only learn to walk in that favor.

It is too often true that Christians experience far less than God's best for them. However, God's promises are meant especially for

Christians. Therefore, the place to start is with your relationship with God.

It has been said that the entire Bible speaks of relationship, ours with God. That relationship starts with the new birth in Christ (John 3:16) which must be followed by spiritual growth. For there to be much spiritual growth, you also need to receive the baptism with the Holy Spirit from Jesus (Luke 11:13). The Holy Spirit produces the spiritual nature of God in you (Galatians 5:22, 23). As you receive the spiritual nature of God, your old nature with its hopelessness (Galatians 5:19-21) is replaced. To be victorious in Christ, you also need God's armor and armament for life's battles (Ephesians 6:10-18). Finally, you need to begin practicing God's "spiritual laws" or "principles."

Examine Christ's offer of "treasure in heaven" to the rich, young ruler (Matthew 19:21), or His offer of "living water" to the woman at the well (John 4:1-15). Pray for and establish a new vision of what your lifestyle and relationships are to be like under God's authority.

As you study, learn and experience God's full counsel for you, your life takes on victory rather than defeat. You walk in faith and its results rather than constantly being defeated by the circumstances of life. Your prayers will become prayers of faith (and sure hope) rather than hopeless prayers.

God has people to help you no matter what your needs—physical, spiritual, emotional, marital, or whatever. Contact a local Bible-believing, Spirit-filled fellowship of Christians, such as The Full Gospel Business Men's or Women's Aglow Fellowships. There are churches available in most communities where people are experiencing the victory you need. They have discovered the God of hope (Psalm 71). He is only a prayer away.

As You Pray

Give thanks and praise to God who, in spite of problems, gives hope to the hopeless.

References/Homework

Romans 4:18-25	The faith of Abraham
Psalm 23	God's assurances
2 Corinthians 4:7-9	Victorious hope
Romans 5:5	Hope does not disappoint

Notes

_____

_____

_____

_____

_____

_____

_____

_____

HUMILITY

God lifts up the humble person. He will be highly respected by his fellowman as he is with God.

Humility is the opposite of pride. If you are humble, you consider yourself the servant of others. You do not feel or act superior to others and you are not a respector of persons.

The Lord promotes whom He will. He puts down one person and raises another. If you are promoted, you should not proudly boast (Psalm 75:5-7). The one who would be first should be the servant of all, for "the last shall be first, and the first last" (Matthew 20:16).

What Scripture Says

"Humble yourselves in the sight of the Lord, and he shall lift you up" (James 4:10).

"For even the Son of man came not to be ministered unto, but to minister, and to give his life a ransom for many" (Mark 10:45).

"Before destruction the heart of man is haughty, and before honour is humility" (Proverbs 18:12).

"A man's gift maketh room for him, and bringeth him before great men" (Proverbs 18:16).

"A man that hath friends must show himself friendly: and there is a friend that sticketh closer than a brother" (Proverbs 18:24).

Humility vs. Pride

Pride is the first product of our natural sin of self-consciousness. Every problem we have can be traced to it. Eve was prideful when she yielded to the temptation to satisfy her lack of the knowledge of good and evil. Job's sin was pride. When he repented of it, God restored to him all he had lost.

You may be on a "head trip" and not realize it. If you are proud, your behavior will reflect it. Do you talk "down" or "up" to people rather than "to" them? Do you always want to have your way in the affairs of your life? Do you seek to be blessed by others rather than seeking ways to bless them? If so, you need to learn humility.

It can be argued that pride in any form is sin. Yet we are often taught to be "proud." For example, military slogans which are designed to promote "esprit de corps" feed the ego and enhance pride. Such pride seems to be a good thing.

Yet how can a person be proud and humble at the same time? Upon closer examination, you'll find that pride—no matter what form it takes—leads to a self-seeking life where relationships with other people and with God suffer.

God has provided the answer to our inborn sin of pride. It is the fruit of the Spirit, which includes meekness. Humility is one aspect of meekness. The meek shall inherit the earth (cf. Beatitudes), not the proud.

So how do you replace pride with humility? First, you need salvation and the baptism with the Holy Spirit. And you must repent of pride. When Christ reigns in your life, you are in the right relationship with God and other people. To be free from the sin of pride, repent and call on the Lord for forgiveness. Ask Him to come into your life in all His fullness. Commit your life to Him. Ask Him to baptize you with the Holy Spirit. The Holy Spirit can replace your fleshly nature with the nature of God.

Renew your mind as you strive for humility. Allow the fruit of the Spirit (the nature of God) to be produced within you (Galatians 5:22, 23). Become all that you can become in the Lord.

As You Pray

Seek the Lord as to how to pray. Expect the Spirit to reveal areas of your life of which you need to repent. Rejoice in God's forgiveness of sin.

Pray for the fruit of the Spirit. Rejoice in the sure knowledge that God will give you this desire of your heart.

HUMILITY

References/Homework

James 4:6, 10	Rewarding of humility
Proverbs 18:12	Honor is the result of humility
Philippians 2:5-11	Christ's example (cf. John 13:1-17)
Mark 10:45	Christ's example as a servant
Matthew 16:24	Christ's admonition to forget self
Isaiah 57:15; 66:2	The humble dwell with God
Matthew 20:16, 26-28	The last will be first
Luke 14:11	Humility brings greatness

Notes

_____

_____

_____

_____

_____

_____

_____

_____

INCEST/MOLESTATION

The sin of incest is impure sexual intercourse between close family members, whether involving two adults or an older and a younger family member. It is a crime of perverse sexual behavior.

Molestation is when any older person, family member or not, sexually abuses or molests a younger, underaged person. Obvious examples would be adult-adolescent or parent-child sexual activity. The legal age of consent is normally considered in determining whether an act is one of molestation.

Biblically, any sexual behavior outside of marriage is sinful behavior.

What Scripture Says

"None of you shall approach to any that is near of kin to him, to uncover their nakedness: I am the Lord. . . . For whosoever shall commit any of these abominations, even the souls that commit them shall be cut off from among their people" (Leviticus 18:6, 29).

"And the man that lieth with his father's wife . . . his daughter-in-law. . . take a wife and her mother . . . take his sister, his father's daughter, or his mother's daughter . . . it is a wicked thing; and they shall be cut off in the sight of their people . . . he shall bear his iniquity" (Leviticus 20:11, 12, 14, 17).

"For John had said unto Herod, It is not lawful for thee to have thy brother's wife" (Mark 6:18).

"It is reported commonly that there is fornication among you, and such fornication as is not so much as named among the Gentiles, that one should have his father's wife. . . . deliver such an one unto Satan for the destruction of the flesh, that the spirit may be saved in the day of the Lord Jesus" (1 Corinthians 5:1, 5).

"But put ye on the Lord Jesus Christ, and make not provision for the flesh, to fulfill the lusts thereof" (Romans 13:14).

"There hath no temptation taken you but such as is common to man: but God is faithful, who will not suffer you to be tempted above that ye are able; but will with the temptation also make a way to escape, that ye may be able to bear it" (1 Corinthians 10:13).

If You Are the Abuser

Incest or sexual molestation is a sin from which you need to be free. You must repent! The habits or life patterns that you are following need changing. Ask God to forgive and set you free from the temptations.

Be bold and ask your pastor or a Christian counselor to pray with you and help you to overcome the problem. Ask them to pray in agreement with you and with God's Word that you may be forgiven and delivered from incest or molestation.

If you have not been reborn spiritually, you can be. You can be clean again. Regardless of this sin or any other (sin is sin, with none greater than the other), call on the Lord to save, forgive and cleanse you and to come into your heart, right now (1 John 1:8, 9; Romans 10:13; John 1:12). You can have the new life God has for you (2 Corinthians 5:17).

If You Were Abused

The trauma of your experiences need not ruin your life from now on. You may feel guilty because you may have consented to incest or allowed yourself to be molested. Or perhaps you and/or the abuser were Christians when the sin took place. Nevertheless, God will forgive you.

Many who have been victims (willingly or not) of incest or molestation have memories which deny them the freedom to live without hate, bitterness and resentment, fear and/or a desire for revenge. Yet you can be free and even find forgiveness for the abuser in your heart. Jesus and Stephen, at the time of their deaths, were both able to forgive those who executed them. Both looked to heaven and asked God to forgive the sins of those who were guilty. Especially if you are a Christian, you have authority and influence with God concerning remittance of sin or retention of sin (John 20:23). God

144

will listen to your prayer. Just remember that Jesus came to forgive rather than to condemn (John 3:16).

It is important that you forgive your abuser. Also, ask God to forgive him or her. This releases God's forgiveness. Although it is often hard to forgive and forget, you can *REMEMBER WITH FOR-GIVENESS*.

Finally, God will even release you from the pain of the memories. As you remember the ordeal of the incest or molestation, allow the Holy Spirit, in power and healing, to cleanse your mind and give you God's peace. Begin to praise and thank God who releases you and lifts your burdens (Ephesians 5:20; 1 Thessalonians 5:17; Psalm 22:3; Romans 8:28). Sacrifice praise to God, your Great Physician (Hebrews 13:15), until you have peace and joy in your heart and liberty in your spirit. When that becomes a reality to you, you will know that you are free and new in the Lord.

If You Discovered Abuse

Both the abuser and the victim need help. You may need help also if you are a close friend or relative. If you are a born-again Christian, pray before you do anything. Remember that you may not know every circumstance. The abuse may have ended. If so, a different type of help may now be needed.

You probably should not try to decide what to do alone. It may be that you should seek the counsel of a minister in confidence. Ask for confidentiality if you desire. Act when you are sure of God's leading. Be sure you understand the consequences of any action you may decide to take. Whatever the Lord shows you to do, remember you can and should intercede in prayer, if a Christian, for everyone concerned. Remember that it is not vengeance, but help that is needed.

As You Pray

Whether you are the guilty one, the victim, a family member, friend or other, pray for God's forgiveness for all concerned. Pray for the wisdom to know what to do now. Thank and praise God and honor Him as the Problem Solver. Dwelling upon the problem honors Satan

INCEST/MOLESTATION

and the sin. Boldly, in Jesus' name, rebuke incest and perversion. Renounce the sin and the satanic influence over everyone involved.

References/Homework

Acts 15:20; 1 Corinthians 5:1, 6; 6:13-18; 7:2; 1 Thessalonians 4:3	Fornication
Proverbs 2:16-19; 6:20; 7:27; 9:13-18	Adultery
Genesis 19:1-30; Romans 1:18-32	Perversion

Notes

_____

_____

_____

_____

_____

_____

_____

_____

INSOMNIA

Inability to sleep may be accompanied by or result from various burdens such as sickness, financial worries, old age, grief, depression, etc. God's answer to insomnia is through His salvation.

Salvation provides forgiveness of sin, but it also includes health. Because of God's salvation, we can lay ourselves down and sleep, dwelling in safety (Psalm 4:8).

What Scripture Says

"I laid me down and slept; I awakened; for the Lord sustained me" (Psalm 3:5).

"I will both lay me down in peace, and sleep: for thou, Lord, only makest me dwell in safety" (Psalm 4:8).

"It is vain for you to rise up early, to sit up late, to eat the bread of sorrows: for so he giveth his beloved sleep" (Psalm 127:2).

"When thou liest down, thou shalt not be afraid: yea, thou shalt lie down, and thy sleep shall be sweet" (Proverbs 3:24).

"Upon this I awaked, and beheld; and my sleep was sweet unto me" (Jeremiah 31:26).

"Come unto me, all ye that labour and are heavy laden, and I will give you rest" (Matthew 11:28).

To Be Rid of Insomnia

Be aware that the problems associated with insomnia are important. They may include: fear, sickness, financial worries, old age, grief, family problems and demon activity. Each of these problems can be traced to our natural state of sin: "self-consciousness." Self-consciousness is the root cause of every problem you will ever experience in the world, even insomnia.

Anything less than faith, such as fear and worry, is a sin. If you are fearful or worried, you need to repent. God promised rest to those who would come to Him (His beloved). As you cast your cares (obstacles to rest and sleep) upon Him who cares for you, you will have done all you can to remove obstacles to His rest. Your faith in Him to resolve the problems will bring results.

As long as your mind and attention are upon your problem, you are not free from it. Practice the principle of praise, thanking and praising God even in the insomnia (Ephesians 5:20; 1 Thessalonians 5:18). As you show honor and respect to the Problem Solver rather than the problem, you are changing your focus from the problem to Jesus. Minister to the Healer of the problem instead of the problem. Praise and thanksgiving should be offered until victory comes and you are able to sleep.

If you have done the above and you still cannot receive rest and sleep, it may be that you are unable to see beyond the problem and can't minister praise to God and claim God's promises in faith. Whatever the reason, it is time to call for help. Contact your pastor or other Spirit-filled friends. As at least two people agree in prayer, expect God to answer (Matthew 18:19).

God has people anointed with the Holy Spirit who are prepared to intercede for you in your time of need. They are able to bind any power Satan may have over you physically, mentally, and spiritually, and to speak wholeness and healing to you in the authority of Jesus.

As You Pray
Pray in authority and power over every cause of your insomnia. Praise and thank God for victory over sleeplessness and for rest found in Him.

References/Homework

Psalm 3:5	The Lord sustains for sleep
Psalm 4:8	The Lord gives safety for sleep
Psalm 127:2	He gives His beloved sleep
Proverbs 3:24	Sweet sleep promised
Jeremiah 31:3-26	The surety of the Lord gives sweet sleep

Matthew 11:28   Rest promised from labor
Isaiah 26:3   How to receive peace

Study and affirm (confess) the promises listed above. Make praising God the number one priority, rather than begging and struggling to get God to answer your prayer for sleep.

Notes

_____

_____

_____

_____

_____

_____

_____

_____

INTERCESSION

The principle of intercession is that Christians bear one another's burdens, and so fulfill the law of Christ (Galatians 6:2).

In the face of all adversity, sin, illnesses, satanic activity or whatever, God's Word to His people is to intercede (Isaiah 59:16). If we are not interceding, we will find ourselves criticizing, condemning, gossiping and growing bitter, resentful, spiteful and full of hate. This can only lead to trauma, tragedy and destruction.

To intercede in prayer and in the authority of Jesus is one of the greatest needs and obligations we have as Christians.

What Scripture Says

"Likewise the Spirit also helpeth our infirmities: for we know not what we should pray for as we ought: but the Spirit itself maketh intercession for us with groanings which cannot be uttered. And he that searcheth the hearts knoweth what is the mind of the Spirit, because he maketh intercession for the saints according to the will of God. . . . Who is he that condemneth? It is Christ that died, yea rather, that is risen again, who is even at the right hand of God, who also maketh intercession for us" (Romans 8:26, 27, 34).

"I exhort therefore, that, first of all, supplications, prayers, intercessions, and giving of thanks, be made for all men" (1 Timothy 2:1).

"Wherefore he [Christ] is able also to save them to the uttermost that come unto God by him, seeing he ever liveth to make intercession for them" (Hebrews 7:25).

"And he saw that there was no man, and wondered that there was no intercessor: therefore his arm brought salvation unto him; and his righteousness, it sustained him" (Isaiah 59:16).

"Is not this the fast that I have chosen? to loose the bands of wickedness, to undo the heavy burdens, and to let the oppressed go

150

free, and that ye break every yoke? . . . To deal thy bread to the
hungry, and that thou bring the poor that are cast out to thy house?
when thou seest the naked, that thou cover him; and that thou hide
not thyself from thine own flesh?" (Isaiah 58:6, 7).

How to Intercede

The two aspects of intercession are: (1) to intercede with God; and
(2) to stand against Satan, demons, sickness, ungodly circumstances,
etc., in behalf of others. Ezekiel points out that an intercessor must
be willing to feel and bear the burdens of those for whom intercession
is made (Ezekiel 4:4).

These ten principles of intercession are tried and proven as being
effective:

Some Principles for Effective Intercession, by Joy Dawson

1. Praise God for the privilege of engaging in the same won-
derful ministry as the Lord Jesus (Hebrews 7:25).

Praise God for the privilege of cooperating with God in the
affairs of men.

2. Make sure your heart is clean before God, by having given
the Holy Spirit time to convict, should there be any unconfessed
sin (Psalm 66:18; Psalm 139:23, 24).

Check carefully in relation to resentment to anyone (Matthew
6:12; Mark 11:25).

Job had to forgive his friends for their wrong judging of him,
before he could pray effectively for them (Job 42:10).

3. Acknowledge you can't really pray without the direction
and energy of the Holy Spirit (Romans 8:26).

Ask God to utterly control you by His Spirit, receive by faith
that He does, and thank Him (Ephesians 5:18; Hebrews 11:6).

4. Die to your own imaginations, desires, and burdens for
what you feel you should pray (Proverbs 3:5, 6; 28:26; Isaiah
55:8).

5. Deal aggressively with the enemy. Come against him in
the all-powerful name of the Lord Jesus Christ and with the

INTERCESSION

"sword of the Spirit"—the Word of God (James 4:7).

6. Praise God now in faith for the remarkable prayer meeting you're going to have. He's a remarkable God and will do something consistent with His character.

7. Wait before God in silent expectancy, listening for His direction (Psalm 62:5; Micah 7:7; Psalm 81:11-13).

8. In obedience and faith, utter what God brings to your mind, believing (John 10:27).

Keep asking God for direction in relation to whom or what you are praying, expecting Him to give it to you. He will (Psalm 32:8).

Make sure you don't move on to the next subject until you've given God time to discharge all He wants to say to you regarding this particular burden; especially when praying in a group.

Be encouraged from the lives of Moses, Daniel, Paul, and Anna, that God gives revelation to those who make intercession a way of life.

9. If possible have your Bible with you should God want to give you direction or confirmation from it (Psalm 119:105).

10. When God ceases to bring things to your mind to pray for, finish by praising and thanking Him for what He has done, reminding yourself of Romans 11:36.

A WARNING: God knows the weakness of the human heart towards pride, and if we speak of what God has revealed and done in intercession, it may lead to committing this sin.

God shares His secrets with those who are able to keep them. There may come a time when He definitely prompts us to share, but unless this happens we should remain silent (Luke 9:36; 2:19).

As You Pray

Ask God to reveal those needs for which intercession should be made. Thank and praise Him for calling intercessors and equipping them with gifts for lifting burdens and delivering the saints and the needy.

INTERCESSION

References/Homework

Study the Scripture references above.

List those you know who need your intercession. In each case, record the date you begin to intercede as well as the date God begins to answer. As you see God answer, you will build your faith and that of others.

Keep a log (diary) of Scripture, circumstances, words of knowledge, wisdom or prophecy, impressions and thoughts that come to you.

Notes

_____

_____

_____

_____

_____

_____

_____

_____

JUDGMENTAL/
CRITICAL

A judgmental or critical attitude may stem from a strict legalistic interpretation of the Bible, a strict, overbearing conscience or a tendency to be negative in thought, speech and actions. Our natural sinfulness of self-consciousness or pride is at the root of the problem.

If you are frequently judgmental or critical, then you need help in overcoming this attitude. As Paul demonstrated, we should not even be judgmental of ourselves, let alone another. The time for judgment will come and it will be the Lord who will then judge us all (1 Corinthians 4:1-5).

What Scripture Says

"Judge not, that ye be not judged. For with what judgment ye judge, ye shall be judged: and with what measure ye mete, it shall be measured to you again" (Matthew 7:1, 2).

"So when they continued asking him, he lifted up himself, and said unto them, He that is without sin among you, let him first cast a stone at her" (John 8:7).

"Therefore I say unto you, What things soever ye desire, when ye pray, believe that ye receive them, and ye shall have them. And when ye stand praying, forgive, if ye have aught against any: that your Father also which is in heaven may forgive you your trespasses" (Mark 11:24, 25).

"And why beholdest thou the mote that is in thy brother's eye, but perceivest not the beam that is in thine own eye?" (Luke 6:41).

"Who art thou that judgest another man's servant? to his own master he standeth or falleth. Yea, he shall be holden up: for God is able to make him stand" (Romans 14:4).

"For we wrestle not against flesh and blood, but against principalities, against powers, against the rulers of the darkness of this world, against spiritual wickedness in high places" (Ephesians 6:12).

How to Overcome

It is possible to develop an attitude of forgiveness and mercy, such as Jesus Himself portrayed and taught (John 8:3-11; Matthew 18:21, 22).

Learn to look with spiritual eyes and see the "glory that is to be revealed" in a person. Pray that the unsaved person will be saved. A new creature whom you can love may thus be born into the Kingdom of God. Then you will see Christ revealed in him.

Continually remind yourself that just as God is not finished with you yet, neither is He finished with anyone else. Meanwhile, remember that "If you have someone on your heart (interceding for them in prayer), he won't get in your hair."

There is a great truth that will help you understand another person toward whom you have been judgmental or critical. It is that we were made by our Creator to complement each other. This is especially true of Christians (Romans 12:5ff.; Ephesians 4:11ff.; 1 Corinthians 12:7ff.). When a fellow Christian irritates you, ask the Lord to show you how he complements you and vice versa. As God reveals to you that person's unique gift, rejoice. You are free to bless each other by manifesting the unique gifts which God has given you.

Similarly, it may be true that a non-Christian, even though not yielded to God, may bless you and others through his God-given gifts (Romans 8:28).

As You Pray

Remind yourself to look at things with spiritual eyes. Trust God for unseen things and know that He is aware of what is happening with a person and circumstances. Leave the results up to Him.

In your authority in Jesus as a Christian, stand against any judgmental or critical spirit. Speak the peace and love of God upon yourself and anyone who may be the object of such an attitude.

JUDGMENTAL/CRITICAL

References/Homework

Colossians 3:1-3   Seek the things of God

Galatians 6:1-3   Bear one another's burdens

A good homework project is to find daily practical ways to be of help to the one you were judging before.

List all the good, praiseworthy traits, accomplishments, etc., you can find about the person(s) toward whom you find yourself being critical or judgmental. Look for opportunities to share them (a few at a time).

Pray for forgiveness when you find yourself being judgmental or critical. Then ask God to forgive the other person(s) who may have annoyed you or others, even as you forgive them. This releases them to God, and He can draw them to Jesus.

Notes

_____

_____

_____

_____

_____

_____

_____

_____

LONELINESS

Loneliness is often accompanied by feelings of worthlessness, crying easily, feeling sorry for yourself, being at "odd-ends" and needing an encouraging word from God.

God has promised never to leave nor forsake His own. To stand alone among men may often be our lot, but you need never stand without God. He desires to be your constant companion, the Holy One who is God of the whole universe (Isaiah 54:1, 5, 6). It is God, the Holy Spirit, who will comfort you and walk alongside you, even in loneliness (John 16:7ff.).

What Scripture Says

"For the mountains shall depart, and the hills be removed; but my kindness shall not depart from thee, neither shall the covenant of my peace be removed, saith the Lord that hath mercy on thee" (Isaiah 54:10).

"Let your conversation be without covetousness; and be content with such things as ye have: for he hath said, I will never leave thee, nor forsake thee. So that we may boldly say, The Lord is my helper, and I will not fear what man shall do unto me" (Hebrews 13:5, 6).

"God is faithful, by whom ye were called unto the fellowship of his Son Jesus Christ our Lord" (1 Corinthians 1:9).

"Behold, I stand at the door, and knock; if any man hear my voice, and open the door, I will come in to him, and will sup with him, and he with me" (Revelation 3:20).

"The Lord is nigh unto them that are of a broken heart; and saveth such as be of a contrite spirit" (Psalm 34:18).

How to Overcome Loneliness

Jesus is your friend; He will stay closer to you than a brother. He came that you might have a life full of meaning, purpose and abundance

LONELINESS

(John 10:10). Recognize the fact that God favors you and will even now lead you out of loneliness and despair and into His abundance.

When you show someone respect, it will bring you respect in return. Similarly, if you offer friendship, you will receive friendship in return. Therefore, it may be up to you to make the first effort to befriend someone. Pray that God will lead you to someone who needs a friend.

Friendship or fellowship with other Christians can do more than dispel your loneliness. It can provide opportunities for you to grow and serve others. Service to others is one of the best ways to overcome loneliness. Otherwise, the bittersweetness of loneliness and self-pity may become your constant diet.

Every Christian has worth in the body of Christ. Every Christian has a service to perform which will benefit the rest of the church. Even if you are a shut-in, you can find another person in similar circumstances who can be a telephone companion. Together, you can share prayer needs and blessings. There are organizations that provide food and other services for shut-ins. If any exist in your area, contact them. They may offer an opportunity for you to provide help and friendship and receive it as well.

If you are a born-again Christian, become a member of a "prayer chain," interceding for others' needs. Your local church should be able to organize a prayer chain, if one is not already in existence.

If you are not born again and/or baptized with the Holy Spirit, call on the Lord Jesus Christ in repentance of sins and ask for forgiveness (Romans 10:13; 1 John 1:8, 9; John 1:12). Ask the Lord to baptize (fill) you with the Holy Spirit as He promised (Luke 11:13). Your new life in Christ is only a prayer away. New life and a renewed mind are necessary for building a meaningful life. Study the Bible daily. Seek fellowship with others who are of the same mind, who desire to grow in the Lord.

As You Pray
Refuse to indulge in self-pity (a product of our natural sin of self-consciousness). Receive the love of God and the glory and witness

158

of the Holy Spirit. Rejoice in praise and thanksgiving in all circumstances. God will work them to your good (Romans 8:28).

References/Homework

Make a list of people you know who need salvation, etc. Claim God's promises for them. Date the first day of each prayer, and when you learn your prayer is answered.

Become a friend to prisoners by writing them letters. Encourage them, but also request their prayers for your concerns.

Pray for all God's people, the peace of Israel, those in authority, etc. In short, become a prayer warrior and get out of the rut of self-pity. The bondage of loneliness will be broken as you find your place in God's Kingdom.

Notes

_____

_____

_____

_____

_____

_____

_____

_____

LOVE

Two problems many people encounter in receiving and expressing love are: (1) an inability to know and experience God's love and to love Him in return, and (2) an inability to love and receive love from others, including enemies, the unlovely and the lovable.

God commends His love to us. He commands us to love Him and our fellowmen. God is love and He stands ready to produce His perfect love within us (Galatians 5:22). We will know we love God when we love our brethren in Christ and our fellowmen, including our enemies (1 John 4:19-21).

What Scripture Says

"But the fruit of the Spirit is love, joy, peace, longsuffering, gentleness, goodness, faith, meekness, temperance: against such there is no law" (Galatians 5:22, 23).

"And hope maketh not ashamed; because the love of God is shed abroad in our hearts by the Holy Ghost which is given unto us" (Romans 5:5).

"As the Father hath loved me, so have I loved you: continue ye in my love. If you keep my commandments, ye shall abide in my love; even as I have kept my Father's commandments and abide in his love. These things have I spoken unto you, that my joy might remain in you, and that your joy might be full. This is my commandment, That ye love one another, as I have loved you. Greater love hath no man than this, that a man lay down his life for his friends" (John 15:9-13).

How to Love and Be Loved

When you are born again of the Spirit of God, your old nature is changed, and God can give you love for others that is greater than normal human love. If you have not been reborn spiritually, call upon

Jesus Christ now. Repent of all sin. Ask His forgiveness and receive it in faith (Romans 10:13; 1 John 1:8, 9; John 1:12). Ask Jesus to also baptize you (fill you) with the Holy Spirit (Luke 11:13).

The Holy Spirit working within you can produce the highest form of love—*agape* love. It is the kind of love God has for you, wherein He loves regardless of whether you love Him in return. It is the love you need in order to love others, regardless of their response to your love.

The substance of genuine *agape* love is not learned, but a product of the Holy Spirit. It is felt emotionally as your heart receives it. You will realize that you also have a genuine love for God and want to be a blessing to Him and for Him. You will feel a sense of oneness toward others that can be described as being one in essence, one in spirit, one in purpose and effort, one emotionally, and even one physically (as with a spouse)—but especially one in the Spirit of God.

The person who said that "love is a feeling you feel when you feel like you are going to have a feeling you've never felt before" was describing love as a heartfelt emotion. But if not acted out, this emotion cannot be labeled true love. In that sense, it is like faith which if not accompanied by the works which establish it, is not true faith. Read Jesus' confrontation with Peter about Peter's love for Him (John 21:15-17); and James' discourse on faith (James 2:17-26).

Yet an act of love is just so much noise unless it comes from a heart filled with love (see 1 Corinthians 13). Pray that the Holy Spirit will give you love, the fruit of the Spirit. Ask for a great love for people in general. Then specifically ask for a great love for a person whom you find difficult to love. It is then that your deliberate act of love will be received and recognized as genuine, not just an empty action.

You possess genuine love for someone when you find yourself with a desire to bless that person. Ask God to show you all the praise-worthy things about that person and how you can bless him. Then look for opportunities to share those praiseworthy things (a few at a time) and to bless the person. You will soon discover that you genuinely love the person and can soon expect him to love you.

LOVE

How to Overcome Barriers

Barriers to love include pride, jealousy, conceit, ill-manneredness, irritability, holding grudges, selfishness, evil actions or thoughts, childishness and a "give-up" attitude (1 Corinthians 13). If one or more of these is an obstacle in your life, repent and ask God to forgive you for your feelings and actions. Renounce such attitudes and behavior in your life. Begin to praise and thank God, who will change your life as you ask Him. He will free you from the depression, anxiety, anger, hate or that "queasy," uneasy feeling in the pit of your stomach caused by the thought or presence of a particular person.

As you begin to *appreciate* (praise, honor, encourage) people, you will find yourself becoming a positive, victorious, successful, loving person. When you *depreciate* (find fault with, criticize, etc.) people, you find yourself becoming negative, unloving and unloved. When you are a depreciator, you are often part of the problem rather than part of the solution. People may not desire your company, except those of like attitude.

To overcome lovelessness on your part, ask God to produce within you the character traits of truthfulness, faithfulness, hope, patience, spiritual maturity (1 Corinthians 13), and especially the fruit (qualities) produced by the Holy Spirit (Galatians 5:22, 23). As you find yourself being transformed, and your mind being renewed (Romans 12:2), you will discover that you are able to get along with anyone and also that anyone can get along with you. The reality of love—the love of God within you for Himself and others—will be yours. However, do not demand to receive love before you love or to have your love returned. Let God bring that about. Be faithful in the loving nature that God gives you.

As You Pray

Pray in agreement with God's Word that God will fill you with His love and Holy Spirit. A sample prayer: "Father, I believe You love me. The Scripture says I can love You because You first loved me. I thank You for Your love. Fill my heart in a greater way than You ever have before. Fill me with the Holy Spirit and love. Help me to grow in Your love and let me show Your love to all around me. Thank you, Father. In Jesus' name. Amen."

References/Homework
Read *Love Is Now,* Pete Gillquist.
Read the entire book of 1 John.

1 Corinthians 13:4-8	Characteristics associated with love
John 3:16	God's love revealed
1 John 4:7-14	God's love explained
Revelation 1:5	Christ's love is forever
Ephesians 2:4, 5	God's love unearned
Matthew 22:37, 38	Christ's command to love
John 13:34, 35	Love for each other proves we are God's people
Matthew 5:43, 44	Love for enemies enjoined

Notes

_____

_____

_____

_____

_____

_____

_____

_____

_____

LUST

Lust is desiring *anything* in a compelling, cunning, luring manner. It is a term that encompasses all manner of fleshly desire, whether physical or intellectual (1 John 2:16). Accompanied by pride (a sense of your own importance), lust is a product of your natural sinful state of being (self-consciousness).

Paul lists several "works of the flesh," which result from yielding to lusts and pride. He states "that they which do such things shall not inherit the kingdom of God" (Galatians 5:19-21). The Bible says that through the help of Jesus, however, we can rise above our human nature with its lusts.

What Scripture Says

"This I say then, *Walk in the Spirit,* and ye shall not fulfill the lust of the flesh. For the flesh lusteth against the Spirit, and the Spirit against the flesh: and these are contrary the one to the other; so that ye cannot do the things that ye would. But if ye be led of the Spirit, ye are not under the law" (Galatians 5:16-18).

"For all that is in the world, the lust of the flesh, and the lust of the eyes, and the pride of life, is not of the Father, but is of the world" (1 John 2:16).

"Let not sin therefore reign in your mortal body, that ye should not obey it in the lusts thereof" (Romans 6:12).

"But the fruit of the Spirit is love, joy, peace, long-suffering, gentleness, goodness, faith [faithfulness], meekness, temperance [self-control]: against such there is no law" (Galatians 5:22, 23).

Overcoming Lust

You can trace every problem in your life back to your natural sinful state of self-consciousness, from which come fleshly and intellectual lust and pride. No matter what form self-consciousness takes, be

164

aware of the fact that Satan constantly appeals to it. Compare Adam, Eve, and Jesus as they faced temptations which appealed to their self-consciousness and the lust of the flesh. Christ gives you a new, changed nature. And the baptism with the Holy Spirit will give you the ability to overcome self-consciousness and the sins of lust and pride in your life.

As long as you live in the flesh, you will be aware of fleshly appetites. Your human nature is not destroyed as a result of your salvation. Rather, your human nature is atoned for and pardoned. You still need control over lust and pride, which you can obtain by praying for forgiveness of your sin and the fruit of the Spirit, "temperance" (or self-control). With self-control you gain control over lust, rather than letting lust continue to control you (Galatians 5:22, 23; 1 Corinthians 9:25, 27).

You can be in bondage to lust to the extent that your thoughts and activities are constantly directed by it. This is often the case with sexual lust. Constant thinking or fantasizing about fornication and adultery is sin (Matthew 5:28). To be free, you must repent and renounce the lust. Ask for God's forgiveness and also for the Holy Spirit, through whom comes the ability to overcome temptation. God is faithful and will forgive your sin (1 John 1:8, 9). There is no sin so bad that He won't cleanse. The most scarlet of sins He will make "white as snow" (Isaiah 1:18).

A person's spirit is fed by what he honors. The Bible says that what you sow is what you will reap. Rather than sow to lust, sow to the Lord, the one who replaces lust with something better.

Diligently practice praising God. When you minister praise to Him, the "Overcomer," you are not ministering to your lust. God then ministers peace from lust or any other temptation (Isaiah 26:3).To praise Him is to show honor and respect to Him. Praise ministers to God. He ministers to you (1 Samuel 2:30b). Minister praise to Him until you receive peace from the temptations you face.

You will also find the ability to overcome lust as you meditate upon God's Word. Psalm 119:11 says, "Thy Word have I hid in mine heart, that I might not sin against thee." As you read the Scriptures and meditate upon them daily, be assured of having victory over lust or

LUST

anything else which might tend to separate you from the Father. God's Word will keep you from sin, or sin will keep you from God's Word.

As You Pray

Praise and thank God for sending His Son, Jesus Christ, to help you rise above your fleshly lusts. Pray that His perfection will be your perfection, and that His holiness will be your holiness. Claim victory over lust, in the name and by the power of Jesus Christ.

References/Homework

Galatians 5, 6	Freedom and help in Christ
Romans 13:9ff.	Correct behavior is rewarded
1 Timothy 6:9, 10	Lust for money
2 Timothy 2:22, 23	Flee from evil thoughts

Notes

_____

_____

_____

_____

_____

_____

_____

_____

MARITAL RELATIONS

Marital problems strike at the heart of society. Families are destroyed. Entire generations to come are affected. Today many families face the anguish of a marriage on the verge of breaking up. Conflict and disagreement have become a way of life.

Yet God's ideal is that two shall become one flesh (Genesis 2:24) and remain bound together until death (Romans 7:2; 1 Corinthians 7:10, 11; Mark 10:9). If your marriage is on shaky ground there are steps you can take to save it. Similarly, you can intercede on behalf of a friend or family member who is experiencing marital difficulties.

What Scripture Says

"Whoso findeth a wife findeth a good thing, and obtaineth favour of the Lord" (Proverbs 18:22).

"I will therefore that the younger women marry, bear children, guide the house, give none occasion to the adversary to speak reproachfully" (1 Timothy 5:14).

"Marriage is honourable in all, and the bed undefiled: but whoremongers and adulterers God will judge" (Hebrews 13:4).

"But I say unto you, that whosoever shall put away his wife, saving for the cause of fornication, causeth her to commit adultery: and whosoever shall marry her that is divorced committeth adultery" (Matthew 5:32).

"What therefore God hath joined together, let not man put asunder" (Mark 10:9).

"Let the husband render unto the wife due benevolence: and likewise also the wife unto the husband. The wife hath not power of her own body, but the husband: and likewise also the husband hath not the power of his own body, but the wife" (1 Corinthians 7:3, 4).

MARITAL RELATIONS

How to Save Your Marriage

First of all, you need to be born again. As a natural, non-spiritual person, you can't know or receive spiritual things, and you are in a spiritual battle for life and its roots—the family. Ask God to baptize you with the Holy Spirit. You need to know the voice, authority and power of God.

God may show you that you have a problem accepting your spouse as he or she is. Perhaps you are unforgiving or unsubmissive toward each other. God is ready to listen to your prayers of repentance. And as a Christian, there are steps of intercession you can follow.

As You Pray

Pray, binding Satan (Matthew 18:18). He is a liar and a deceiver and is bent on destroying marriages. Authoritatively and forcefully command him to be bound, to leave and not return. God has given you that authority as a born-again, Spirit-filled believer. Turn your attention from your problems, hurts, worries and anxieties to God. Give Him preeminence. Minister thanksgiving and praise to God for solving the problem. He knows your need and is already answering as you pray.

Thank God for producing the fruit of the Spirit: love, joy, peace, goodness, kindness, patience, faithfulness, meekness, and self-control (Galatians 5:22, 23) in each family member. Ask God to send angels to minister in the situation (Hebrews 1:14). Thank and praise Him for doing it.

If you fast in behalf of your marriage, interceding in prayer and standing against Satan and with God for the spiritually weak person, God has promised to honor such a fast and repair the breach (Isaiah 58:6-12).

Claim God's favor (Psalm 103:8). Thank and praise the Lord for making His face shine upon both of you and being gracious to you (Numbers 6:25). He is grounding you and letting your spiritual roots go deep. He is keeping you according to His power working in you (Ephesians 3:17-20). Therefore, at each instance of prayer, praise God continually for restoring and blessing your marriage (Hebrews 13:15).

What Next?

Seek out a warm, loving church fellowship if you are not already attending one. Choose a caring prayer partner in whom you can have confidence. Pray together frequently. Agree together for the needs of you and your spouse (Matthew 18:19). Remember, you don't need pity or someone who will agree with you that you are right and your spouse is wrong. You need someone to intercede with you in behalf of your marriage.

Seek out a pastor for counseling and continued prayer. Be faithful to the Lord no matter what happens. God loves you. He wants to loose His blessing on you and your spouse so that you may be drawn to Jesus—just because He loves you. Offer thanks and praise to God for smoothing out the rough places.

References/Homework

Read *Divorce,* John Murray; *The Christian Family,* Larry Christenson.

Duties of husbands and wives:

Genesis 2:23, 24	Esther 1:20
Proverbs 5:18	Proverbs 31
Ecclesiastes 9:9	1 Corinthians 7:10
Ephesians 5:22-25	1 Peter 3:1, 7
1 Timothy 3:11	

Make a list of all the things for which you can honestly praise your spouse. Each day share five of these with your spouse. Do this instead of criticizing for at least one week. Continue until your list runs out. In doing so you will be appreciating your spouse versus depreciating him or her with criticism, negativism, etc. Watch God work as His love fills your hearts.

Notes

_____

_____

_____

MENTAL ILLNESS

Mental illness is a part of the curse of the law and is often a result of sin and disobedience to God (Deuteronomy 28:15, 28). Sometimes demonic activity is involved (Matthew 17:14-21), or possibly actual physiological damage. But the Word of God promises a Christian a sound mind.

What Scripture Says

"For God hath not given us the spirit of fear; but of power, and of love, and of a sound mind" (2 Timothy 1:7).

"Thou wilt keep him in perfect peace, whose mind is stayed on thee: because he trusteth in thee" (Isaiah 26:3).

"Finally, brethren, whatsoever things are true, whatsoever things are honest, whatsoever things are just, whatsoever things are pure, whatsoever things are lovely, whatsoever things are of good report; if there be any virtue, and if there be any praise, think on these things" (Philippians 4:8).

"The Spirit of the Lord is upon me, because he hath anointed me to preach the gospel to the poor; he hath sent me to heal the broken-hearted, to preach deliverance to the captives, and recovering of sight to the blind, to set at liberty them that are bruised, to preach the acceptable year of the Lord" (Luke 4:18, 19).

"And be not conformed to this world: but be ye transformed by the renewing of your mind, that ye may prove what is that good, and acceptable, and perfect, will of God" (Romans 12:2).

Sin and Mental Illness

Unrepentance for sin and other irresponsible behavior should be the first areas of your life to examine when you are suffering emotional problems or mental illness.

Irresponsible behavior (works of the flesh—Galatians 5:19-21) can result in some fearful consequences: suicidal tendencies, fearfulness, compulsive actions seemingly beyond your control, rebelliousness, drug involvement, etc.

If people are accusing you of unacceptable remarks or behavior, you may also be realizing that something may be wrong. You may be doing things which you know are wrong, and want to stop but feel unable to do so. If so, have you been reading occult material such as horoscopes, Eastern religion or cult-oriented literature, literature about witchcraft or black magic, Satan worship and other non-biblical religious literature?

Physical or Demonic Causes

Physical brain damage may be caused by sinful behavior, such as when immorality causes a venereal disease. Or an auto accident, a war wound, drug abuse, etc., may cause brain damage or mental disorientation. In such cases, competent medical help is often needed. Consult a pastor or other Christian counselor for help and possible referral.

If you suspect demonic influences, a pastor or other competent Christian counselor should be consulted to help you determine what your need is and to minister directly to your problem. Be careful to not blame every indication of emotional or mental distress upon demon activity. In fact, most such problems are caused by irresponsible, sinful behavior.

How to Overcome

In your effort to help yourself, the first thing you need to do is to call on the Lord Jesus Christ and repent of any sin, including the sin of rebelling against God and His righteousness, not believing His Word, or not wanting to yield your life to Him. Renounce involvement with drugs, occult groups and all irresponsible activities which you know displease God.

God's Word says that if you will repent and ask Him, He will save you from your sins, forgive you and make you a new person (Romans 10:13; 1 John 1:8, 9: John 1:12; 10:9, 10; 3:16). If you haven't done that, do not wait. Do it now and make a total commitment of your life to God. Then, ask Jesus to baptize you with the Holy Spirit (Luke

MENTAL ILLNESS

11:13). The Holy Spirit gives you the ability to overcome sin in your life and to live victoriously in Christ.

You are responsible to God for your own behavior. However, when Jesus ascended back to heaven, He sent the Holy Spirit, whose tasks include giving a Christian the ability to live a full, meaningful, purposeful, and healthy life (John 14; 15-17; 16:7-15).

In any case, contact a Bible-believing ministry or your pastor. Ask for prayer in agreement with you that God will heal you physically, spiritually and mentally, and will deliver you from your problem. As a born-again, Spirit-filled Christian, God's Word will begin to become a reality to you. Join a Spirit-filled fellowship where there is continuing love, counseling and an opportunity for spiritual growth.

As You Pray

Claim God's promises that you will be loosed from all oppression and be set free. Pray for and expect God to move in your life. Agree with God's Word that God is answering your prayer. Thank Him for all that you are experiencing, knowing that He will work it to the good as He promised those who love Him and who are the called according to His purpose (Romans 8:28). Pray in faith that this "mountain" will be removed from you.

References/Homework

2 Timothy 1:7	Holy Spirit gives wisdom, strength, freedom from fear
Philippians 4:8; 2:1-13	God is at work in us
Isaiah 26:3	Peace promised
Ephesians 5:15-21	Carefulness in actions enjoined
Galatians 6:12-14	Carefulness in choosing teachers enjoined
Romans 12:2	God's ways will satisfy
Galatians 3:13	We are free from condemnation and bondage (compare with Deuteronomy 28:15, 28)
Psalm 1:1-3	We are blessed who delight in God's laws

OBEDIENCE/ DISOBEDIENCE

Obedience is the practical acceptance of the authority and will of God. It includes both submitting to Him and then expressing that submission in actions, words and thoughts. To be obedient is to be in agreement with God. To be in agreement with God is to be in a position of power in Christ.

Disobedience is caused by rebellion and distrust of God. To be disobedient is to yield to self-will instead of surrendering to God and desiring His will in all things.

God expects obedience (Deuteronomy 11:26-28). To choose Christ is to choose obedience (John 14:15, 21). To become disobedient is to sin or rebel against God (1 Samuel 15:22, 23).

What Scripture Says

"Behold, I set before you this day a *blessing* and a *curse;* A blessing, if ye obey the commandments of the Lord your God, which I command you this day: And a curse, if ye will not obey the commandments of the Lord your God, but turn aside out of the way which I command you this day, to go after other gods, which ye have not known" (Deuteronomy 11:26-28).

"And Samuel said, Hath the Lord as great delight in burnt offerings and sacrifices, as in obeying the voice of the Lord? Behold . . . rebellion is as the sin of witchcraft, and stubbornness is as iniquity and idolatry. Because thou has rejected the word of the Lord, he hath also rejected thee from being king" (1 Samuel 15:22, 23).

"If ye be willing and obedient, ye shall eat the good of the land" (Isaiah 1:19).

"If ye love me, keep my commandments. . . . He that hath my commandments, and keepeth them, he it is that loveth me: and he that loveth me shall be loved of my Father, and I will love him, and will manifest myself to him" (John 14:15, 21).

"And why call ye me Lord, Lord, and do not the things which I say?" (Luke 6:46).

"But be ye doers of the word, and not hearers only, deceiving your own selves" (James 1:22).

How to Correct the Sin of Disobedience

The following suggestions should help you discover areas of either deliberate or subconscious disobedience to God and to those in authority over you. Begin by asking yourself whether you are obeying God in different areas of your life, such as personal relationships, your behavior, God's lordship in your marriage or job or other areas, personal devotions, etc. Take an honest inventory of your life.

Thank God for areas of disobedience you may discover. Once identified, they can be removed. This will result in new joy and greater faith (Romans 8:28; Ephesians 5:20; 1 Thessalonians 5:18).

Confess the disobedience as sin. Ask God for forgiveness and claim His promise of complete pardon (1 John 1:9). If your act of disobedience involves others who are in authority over you, you must rectify the situation with them. The Bible teaches that we can and should live at peace with ourselves and others. Disobedience to God and those in authority over you can block the joy, blessings and inner peace which God desires for you.

Use your will to relinquish each specific act of disobedience. Denounce even the desire to be disobedient. As Paul did, compel your flesh and its soulishness to obey. The Bible says that as a Christian, you have mighty weapons of warfare which will break down walls of disobedience. Rely on the faith of Jesus and the power of the Holy Spirit.

Plan specific actions. Ask forgiveness of others, make amends where needed. Seek the fruit of the Spirit: Love, joy, peace, goodness, kindness, meekness, faithfulness, patience and self-control (Galatians 5:22, 23). As each of these qualities develops in you, you will find not only the sin of disobedience fading, but other sins as well.

174

OBEDIENCE/DISOBEDIENCE

As You Pray

Pray that the fruit of the Spirit, faithfulness to God and other people, be produced within you (Galatians 5:22, 23).

Thank and praise God for revealing your disobedience to you and for giving you meekness (submissiveness) and love for Him and others—even your enemies. Rejoice in your new freedom and joy in the Lord as you realize that you are free from the bondage of disobedience.

References/Homework

1 John 5:2, 3	Test of obedience and love
Colossians 3	Admonition to emulate Jesus
Psalm 51	David's example of new obedience to God

1. Take a piece of paper and draw a vertical line down the center.

2. To the left of the line list the areas in which you have been disobedient.

3. To the right of the line list the alternatives of obedience. Begin to act on the alternatives, forming new life patterns.

Notes

_____

_____

_____

_____

_____

_____

_____

_____

_____

OCCULT

Included in things of the occult are precognition (or fortune-telling), ESP, telepathy, clairvoyance, automatic writing, ouija boards and other games that claim a magical or demonically spiritual orientation, astrology, horoscopes, tea leaf reading, palmistry, techniques of mind expansion, drugs, hypnotism, mind control, transcendental meditation, yoga, sorcery or witchcraft, physical phenomena, telekinesis, levitation, astral projection, spiritism or spiritualism, seances and satanism, animal and human sacrifices, animism, etc.

In natural and spiritual history, a society degenerates according to a pattern. It goes from a diminishing God-centered spiritual life to legalism, to materialism, to liberalism, to seeking life's answers outside the Bible, and then to spiritism, couched in the occult. Occultism often involves drugs, idolatry, and sexual perversion.

Even as we are besieged with the many forms and avenues of satanic influence, we have the absolute authority, through our Lord Jesus Christ, to bind the powers of darkness and dispel them. They must do our bidding as we speak "in the name of Jesus" (Matthew 16:19; 18:18; Mark 16:17; Luke 10:18, 19; Ephesians 1:17-23).

What Scripture Says
"Thou shalt not suffer a witch to live" (Exodus 22:18). This was the Old Testament means of eliminating a practice and manifestation of the enemy, Satan.

"There shalt not be found among you any one that maketh his son or his daughter to pass through the fire, or that useth divination, or an observer of times, or an enchanter, or a witch, or a charmer, or a consulter with familiar spirits, or a wizard, or a necromancer. For all that do these things are an abomination unto the Lord: and because of these abominations the Lord thy God doth drive them out from before thee. Thou shalt be perfect with the Lord thy God" (Deuteronomy 18:10-13).

"And I will come near to you to judgment; and I will be a swift witness against the sorcerers, and against the adulterers, and against false swearers, and against those that oppress the hireling in his wages, the widow, and the fatherless, and that turn aside the stranger from his right, and fear not me, saith the Lord of hosts" (Malachi 3:5).

"Now the works of the flesh are manifest, which are these; adultery, fornication, uncleanness, lasciviousness, idolatry, witchcraft, hatred, variance, emulations, wrath, strife, seditions, heresies, envyings, murders, drunkenness, revellings, and such like: of the which I tell you before, as I have also told you in time past, that they which do such things shall not inherit the kingdom of God" (Galatians 5:19-21).

"The Spirit of the Lord is upon me, because he hath anointed me to preach the gospel to the poor; he hath sent me to heal the brokenhearted, to preach deliverance to the captives, and recovering of sight to the blind, to set at liberty them that are bruised, to preach the acceptable year of the Lord" (Luke 4:18, 19).

"But the fearful, and unbelieving, and the abominable, and murderers, and whoremongers, and sorcerers, and idolators, and all liars, shall have their part in the lake which burneth with fire and brimstone: which is the second death" (Revelation 21:8).

How to Be Free

If you have been involved in occultism in any form—even if you have only read about it—renounce any specific occult activity and occultism in general. Repent of your belief in and practice of the occult. It is sin and an abomination to God. Ask forgiveness of God. He will deliver you, save you and lead you into truth (Romans 10:13; 1 John 1:8, 9; John 1:12; Romans 6:23; John 16:13).

You need the baptism with the Holy Spirit to have an overcoming victorious life. The Holy Spirit warns you concerning what is of sin and what is of God (John 16:7-11). By faith repent and put your faith in Christ for salvation (Romans 10:9, 10, 13). By faith, also ask the

Lord to baptize you (fill you) with the Holy Spirit (Luke 11:13). It is the Holy Spirit who gives the ability to stay free from the deception and spiritual bondage of occultism.

Replace occult books, magazines, etc., with the Bible and Christian reading matter. Seek Christian fellowship and practice Christian living. A complete break with occultism is necessary.

If you have attempted to pray to God, change your life, or cease occult or associated activities, but have discovered an inability to do so, you may need further help. God has equipped Christians to minister to you. You do not have to remain in spiritual bondage. Contact your local pastor to help you locate a Christian counselor whose ministry includes deliverance from spiritual bondage.

As You Pray

As you ask forgiveness and God's help, thank and praise Him for His assurance of deliverance from the occult. As you commit your life to God, ask Him to lead you to those Christians who are capable of helping you in your need.

References/Homework

"Saturate" yourself with Scriptures. Begin with the Gospel according to John. Then read the rest of the New Testament. Acquire a Bible study guide. Get into a Holy Spirit-led fellowship. Learn about Jesus and get serious with God. You will recognize the counterfeit when you know the real God.

Read *Defeated Enemies,* Corrie Ten Boom; *Demons in the World Today,* Merrill Unger; *The Devil's Alphabet,* Kurt Koch; and *His Infernal Majesty,* Dave Breese.

Deuteronomy 18:9-22	Occult abominations
Acts 13:6-12	Example of God's power over occultism
Jeremiah 27:9, 10	Occultism exposed

PARENT/CHILD

The desire of every parent and child is to find happiness in life and to live in a loving, happy family relationship. However, conflict, rebellion, lack of discipline, confusion and anxiety often mar the peace and happy relationships that should reign in the family. The Christian who is seeking how to effect "rightness" in relationships is often the one who must first reach out to the other family members.

God's desire is that all should come to a knowledge of the truth, be saved, be empowered for life and grow up into the fullness of Christ. This requires self-discipline and the submitting of oneself to others. In the case of children, the submission is first of all to their parents in the Lord. Always, whether parent or child, one is to honor and to prefer the other above self (Romans 12:10).

What Scripture Says

"Observe and hear all these words which I command thee, that it may go well with thee, and with thy children after thee for ever, when thou doest that which is good and right in the sight of the Lord thy God" (Deuteronomy 12:28).

"The just man walketh in his integrity: his children are blessed after him" (Proverbs 20:7).

"Children, obey your parents in the Lord: for this is right. Honour thy father and mother; which is the first commandment with promise; That it may be well with thee, and thou mayest live long on the earth" (Ephesians 6:1-3).

"Children, obey your parents in all things: for this is well pleasing unto the Lord" (Colossians 3:20).

What to Do

Your first need as a parent/child is for salvation and the baptism with the Holy Spirit. Ask Jesus to save you and fill you with His Holy

PARENT/CHILD

Spirit. As a Spirit-filled Christian who is manifesting the fruit of the Spirit—love, joy, peace, kindness, goodness, meekness, faithfulness, patience and self-control—you will be better equipped by God to help the non-Christian family member (Galatians 5:22, 23). You will find yourself more and more able to minister discipline, love, peace, orderliness, etc., in the home. These qualities will help you to be a better example for the good in the family.

The promise of Acts 16:31 is that all who believe in Jesus, along with their households, shall be saved. Claim and act upon the assurance of the fulfillment of this promise.

If you are a Christian child in the home of your parents, the same promise applies. In obeying and respecting your parents, you are obeying and respecting the order God has placed in the home. God's promise is that your testimony will work to draw your parents, brothers and sisters to Jesus for salvation. To disobey your parents is to disobey God, and that brings disorder, confusion and anxiety.

As a Christian parent, you must set a godly example and be responsible for the training and disciplining of your child in the ways of the Lord (Deuteronomy 6:6, 7; Hebrews 12:5, 6, 11). In so doing, you are expressing God's love to your children which will bring them to a place of accepting Jesus Christ into their lives.

There are spiritual principles that can make the difference in how God works in your affairs. One principle is to minister praise to God, giving God pre-eminence in all matters and in relationships. When one ministers to God, God ministers in return (1 Samuel 2:30).

Another principle is that of intercession. As you intercede for your children (or parents), be reminded of God's promises to bring about salvation within every member of the family. Thank and praise Him for doing so. An intercessor stands as proxy before God in behalf of the persons for whom he is praying. He also does spiritual warfare against Satan and his wiles (Ephesians 6:12). As you pray in intercession, you bear the burdens of those prayed for. As you bear those burdens, you will have a better understanding of the person(s) which will lead to a greater love for them. Where there is love, relationships get closer and more loving. As love reigns, and as intercession is made, discipline, order in the home, and peace and joy in the family are sure to follow.

As You Pray

Ask God to give you a great love for your children (or parents). Ask Him to help you see all their praiseworthy traits. Ask for ways to bless them, thus building them up by appreciation, rather than criticizing and depreciating them. Thank and praise God for giving you forgiveness toward them and the same to them for you. Thank Him for His love, praising Him in the sure knowledge that He can and will restore relationships between family members.

References/Homework

Read *The Christian Family,* Larry Christenson.

Philemon   Relationships restored in Christ
Isaiah 58   Fasting to restore relationships

Guidance for parents:
Proverbs 13:24; 19:18; 29:15
Hebrews 12:6-10
Luke 11:11-13
Colossians 3:21
Ephesians 6:4

Guidance for children:
Ephesians 6:1-3
Colossians 3:20

Notes

_____

_____

_____

_____

PEACE

Are you overwrought with inner conflict, fear, overwhelming temptation, anxiety, nervous tension, insomnia or anything that is robbing you of your peace? If so, you need to call on Jesus, the Prince of Peace. Peace is a product of the Holy Spirit's actions (Galatians 5:22). It comes as you give pre-eminence (focus of attention) to the Prince of Peace (Isaiah 26:3).

What Scripture Says

"He that dwelleth in the secret place of the most High shall abide under the shadow of the Almighty" (Psalm 91:1).

"Thou wilt keep him in perfect peace, whose mind is stayed on thee: because he trusteth in thee" (Isaiah 26:3).

"Be careful for nothing; but in every thing by prayer and supplication with thanksgiving let your requests be made known unto God" (Philippians 4:6).

"Therefore take no thought . . . for your heavenly Father knoweth that ye have need. . . . But seek ye first the kingdom of God, and his righteousness; and all [your needs] shall be added unto you" (Matthew 6:31-33).

How to Find Peace

The primary need for all people is salvation of their souls. When the Prince of Peace dwells within us, the Holy Spirit is able to produce His peace within us (Romans 10:13; 1 John 1:9; John 1:12).

Upon asking Christ for the baptism (filling) of the Holy Spirit, you are eligible for all that God offers those who trust in Him. It is the Holy Spirit who empowers you for service, leads you into truth, comforts you and works mightily within you to give you victory over every situation of life which would rob you of your peace in God. Ask for and receive the Holy Spirit now (Luke 11:13).

When worry and wrong actions or attitudes are present, faith is absent. Born-again, Spirit-filled Christians have received the spirit of adoption. We know our Father in such an intimate way, and are known by Him, that we can call Him "Abba" or "Daddy." The inheritance of His children is ours. Peace is included in that inheritance.

God's Word promises that we are to be recipients of the fruit (qualities) of the Holy Spirit. Peace is one of those qualities (Galatians 5:22).

Gaining peace is often a matter of changing our priorities. Honor and respect God instead of worrying over your lack of peace (Isaiah 26:3). When you praise Him, you enthrone Him instead of the thoughts and emotions that take away your peace (Psalm 22:3). As you bless Him with your praise, He will bless you with His peace.

No matter what may disturb you and cause your sense of well-being and peace to flee, you can give thanks and praise to God for it. Be assured that He intends to work even the most unlikely or seemingly impossible situation to the good of those who love Him, who are "called according to His purpose" (Ephesians 5:20; 1 Thessalonians 5:18; Romans 8:28).

Begin to thank and praise God in every need, and especially when you need assurance of His concern and saving power. Continue to honor God in praise until peace comes and joy springs up in your heart (Hebrews 13:15). The joy and peace mean that God accepts your praise.

Finally, transform your thinking and actions. Start by intensively searching the Scriptures regarding freedom in Christ, authority as a Christian and how you can overcome the adversary, Satan. Faithfully attend your church. Study God's Word and spend time daily in prayer and worshipful praise to God. His peace is yours as you seek Him.

As You Pray

In the authority of Jesus, bind demonic spirits. Command them to flee in Jesus' name. Thank and praise God for His peace to you. Minister praise and thanksgiving to God regarding the fruit of the Spirit being given to you. Rejoice in the Lord in all circumstances. He wants to give you the desire of your heart.

PEACE

References/Homework

Read *Peace with God,* Billy Graham.

Romans 5:1-11	We are inheritors of peace
Ephesians 2:14	Christ is our peace
John 14:27	Peace to be claimed
Isaiah 32:17; 48:18	Righteousness and peace
Romans 8:6	Holy Spirit and peace

Notes

_____

_____

_____

_____

_____

_____

_____

_____

PRAISE

The biblical principle of praise is one of the most important principles of the Kingdom of God. When people praise God, miracles happen. Praise shows honor and respect to God. To praise God is to "salute" Him.

When you give honor and respect you will receive honor and respect. When you minister to God by praising Him (Hebrews 13:15), God ministers to you in return (1 Samuel 2:30b). Most importantly, God is enthroned in your praises (Psalm 22:3).

What Scripture Says

"In every thing give thanks: for this is the will of God in Christ Jesus concerning you" (1 Thessalonians 5:18).

"Giving thanks always for all things unto God and the Father in the name of our Lord Jesus Christ" (Ephesians 5:20).

"And we know that all things work together for good to them that love God, to them who are the called according to his purpose" (Romans 8:28).

"But thou art holy, O thou that inhabitest [is enthroned by] the praises of Israel" (Psalm 22:3).

"By him therefore let us offer the sacrifice of praise to God continually, that is, the fruit of our lips giving thanks to his name" (Hebrews 13:15).

"Be it far from me; for them that honour me I will honour . . . " (1 Samuel 2:30b).

Why Praise?

The Old Testament priests ministered to God by offering sacrifices in behalf of the people. We minister to God by offering the sacrifice of praise (Hebrews 13:15).

You should offer sacrifices of praise especially when you face

PRAISE

doubts, obstacles, temptations and the lack of desire to praise. Your praise has been accepted by God when joy and victory come, your burdens lift and peace reigns. Praise God continually in the Spirit so that the Spirit won't be "quenched" (1 Thessalonians 5:19).

You enter into the very presence of God through offering thanksgiving and praise (Psalm 100:4). God honors sincere praise. When you praise Him, you show that you respect Him. Just as you show honor and respect to your elders, superiors, spouse, parents and friends, even more so does God expect you to honor Him.

As You Praise

Praise God in the face of adversity, need and plenty. Even praise Him for parking spaces (before you look for one). In all things, praise Him—especially when you don't feel like it. Persevere in praise. Praise Him in song. Speak out His praise. Praise Him when you awake. Praise Him as you lie down to sleep. Praise Him when you are tempted and continue until the temptation is gone. Praise Him in sickness. He will glorify Himself and raise up the sick. Praise Him for doing it even before it is done.

Give thanks to God and praise Him continually. Expect God to begin ministering to you and give you victory, peace and joy. Expect Him to bless you as you praise Him in your need or in times of victory. As the psalmist said, "PRAISE YE THE LORD."

References/Homework

Read *Prison to Praise, Power in Praise, Praise Works,* and *Answers to Praise,* Merlin Carothers.

Patterns of Praise

Psalms 33:2; 57:8; 150:3-5	With music
Revelation 19:1-10; Psalm 71:8	The mouth
Psalms 63:4; 134:2; 141:2; 47:1	The hands
Psalm 95:6; Ephesians 3:14	Bowing and kneeling
Psalm 135:2	Standing

Acts 3:8; 2 Samuel 6:16	Walking and leaping
Psalm 150:4; 2 Samuel 6:14	Dancing

Results of Praise

Psalm 149:4	Delight of God
Psalm 50:23	Glorifies God
Jude 1:20	Edifies

Notes

_____

_____

_____

_____

_____

_____

_____

_____

_____

PRAYER

Prayer is communicating with God, petitioning Him about needs and problems and honoring Him with thanksgiving and praise.

A Christian addresses the Father directly when he prays, in the authority Jesus delegated to him (John 14:13, 14; Matthew 6:6). A non-Christian needs first to call on Jesus to save him (Romans 10:13). When you have a personal relationship with God, you can be assured that your prayers will be answered (Luke 11:1-13).

What Scripture Says

"Humble yourselves therefore under the mighty hand of God, that he may exalt you in due time" (1 Peter 5:6).

"In whom we have boldness and access with confidence by the faith of him" (Ephesians 3:12).

"Let us come before his presence with thanksgiving, and make a joyful noise unto him with psalms" (Psalm 95:2).

"And he went a little farther, and fell on his face, and prayed, saying, O my Father, if it be possible, let this cup pass from me: nevertheless, not as I will, but as thou wilt" (Matthew 26:39).

"What is it then? I will pray with the spirit, and I will pray with the understanding also: I will sing with the spirit, and I will sing with the understanding also" (1 Corinthians 14:15).

About Prayer

Life-changing prayer occurs when "closeted" with the Father, shutting out all else, keeping your mind on Him (Matthew 6:6). You must give the honor, respect and recognition due God when you come into His presence (Psalm 100:4). To assure that God will answer your prayers, come before Him with a clear conscience and a clean heart. Be aware of these reasons why you may not have your prayers answered: disobedience (Deuteronomy 1:42-45); secret sin (Psalm

66:18); indifference (Proverbs 1:24-28); neglect of mercy (Proverbs 21:13); despising God's law (Proverbs 28:9); blood-guiltiness (Isaiah 1:15); iniquity (Isaiah 59:2); stubbornness (Zechariah 7:13); instability (James 1:6, 7); and self-indulgence (James 4:3).

Take a fearless inventory of your life. Repent of all sin as it is revealed to you. Then, in faith, come to God with your prayers, entering His presence with thanksgiving and praise. Most prayers should consist of thanking God for answering your request, even before you ask anything of Him. He knows what you need and answers before you pray (Isaiah 65:24).

If you do not know how to pray for a particular need, you can pray in the Spirit (in unlearned language) if you have received the baptism with the Holy Spirit. Romans 8:26, 27 gives us understanding of the role of the Holy Spirit in prayer.

Hundreds of books have been written on prayer. Yet it remains misunderstood. Jesus' disciples desired to be taught to pray. Jesus told them to pray continually, but simply, and in faith (Luke 11:1-13).

As You Pray

Offer a prayer of thanksgiving and praise, knowing that God answers prayer. In faith, ask Him for the desires of your heart, knowing that the prayers of a righteous person will be heard (1 John 5:14).

References/Homework

Read *With Christ in the School of Prayer* by Andrew Murray. Study "prayer" with a concordance and your Bible.

John 14:13, 14	In Jesus' name
2 Timothy 1:3	Pure conscience
Isaiah 56:7	Joyfully
1 Thessalonians 5:17;	Continually
Luke 18:1	
Psalm 66:18	With a repentant heart
1 John 5:14, 15;	Believing
Matthew 21:22	

PRAYER

Romans 8:28;
   1 Thessalonians 5:18   In all circumstances

Ephesians 6:18   For all saints
James 5:16   For healing
1 Timothy 2:8   Everywhere

Notes

_____

_____

_____

_____

_____

_____

_____

_____

_____

PRIDE/ORIGINAL SIN

Pride causes you to lift yourself up above God's purpose for you and to think of yourself as above any others (Isaiah 14:13). You may think that you are completely able to take care of things, but problems are never far from you when a high ego is your prominent trait.

Self-consciousness, the basis of pride, is our natural, sinful state of being which causes just about every problem we have. The antidote to pride is to become more conscious of God and others (Matthew 6:33; 22:37, 39). Balance is obtained when you obey the first commandment: to love God; and the second: to love your neighbor as you love yourself.

What Scripture Says

"Before destruction the heart of man is haughty; and before honor is humility" (Proverbs 18:12).

"But he giveth more grace. Wherefore he saith, God resisteth the proud, but giveth grace unto the humble" (James 4:6).

"Every one that is proud in heart is an abomination to the Lord; though hand join in hand, he shall not be unpunished" (Proverbs 16:5).

"Let another man praise thee, and not thine own mouth; a stranger, and not thine own lips" (Proverbs 27:2).

"Humble yourselves therefore under the mighty hand of God, that he may exalt you in due time" (1 Peter 5:6).

God's Alternative

Satan constantly appeals to your basic nature and tempts you through your pride. He tries to deceive you into thinking that it will be all right to sin. But when you are saved, God puts a new nature within you, wherein a love for Him and His righteousness will overrule sin (Romans 8; Colossians 3).

Pride must be repented of. Then pray for a closer more committed walk with the Lord. When submissive to God and those in authority over you, your flesh yields to your walk in the Spirit (Ephesians 5; Galatians 5:19-23; 6). Job was one who seemed to be righteous, but his pride was evident to God (Job 10:7; 12:3; 38:2; 40:1). When Job repented of his pride and prayed for his friends, God restored all that he had lost (Job 40:4, 5; 42:1-6, 10). He became submissive (meek) before the Lord, who then "turned the captivity of Job."

When Eve yielded to the serpent's tempting in the Garden of Eden, she was obeying the cravings of her physical and intellectual appetites and yielded to pride. When Adam listened to Eve, he failed to control his self-conscious nature and, in that act, sinned against God and caused mankind to be cursed. Pride in any form, with the possible exception of "reasonable or justifiable self-respect," is sin. There must be a higher motivation for your attitudes and behavior.

Respond wholeheartedly to God's perfect love. You can be the greatest orator or the most successful person who ever lived, but without the love of God abiding within you, excellent speech is noise and worldly success yields nothing lasting (1 Corinthians 13:1, 2).

Pride causes you to seek your own pleasure and to satisfy your own desires. But it is to God that we are to give offerings of praise and thanksgiving, and it is others that we are to bless. In so doing, God has promised that your every need shall be provided and that honor will be given to you by men, as well as by God Himself (Matthew 6:33; 1 Samuel 2:30b; Psalm 75:6, 7; Luke 6:38).

The higher motivation and the answer to pride is *agape* (charity) LOVE. Charity love is unconditional and requires nothing in return. There is no pride, envy, wrong behavior, self-seeking, easily hurt feelings, impatience, evil thoughts, iniquity, etc., when you have charity love. It is characterized by forbearance and endurance when you are tested. It lasts when all else fails and abides consistently with faith and hope as its companions (1 Corinthians 13).

Charity love is produced by the Holy Spirit. It is not automatically a part of your personality, even after you are born again of the Holy Spirit. Charity love is not something you learn. You can learn to behave as if you have charity love, but the true substance of it must come from the Holy Spirit. Then out of the substance of God-given love can come the behavior which proves its genuineness.

Finally, with love and meekness comes the rest of the fruit of the Spirit: joy, peace, goodness, kindness, patience, faithfulness and self-control (Galatians 5:22, 23). With the fruit of the Spirit (the nature of God) characterizing your life, your original sinful nature (repented of and forgiven) will be under control. You can be authentic in your relationships and God will honor you, as will those whom you honor.

As You Pray

Pray for forgiveness of pride and for God to renew your mind. Seek the mind of Christ in prayer and through Scripture. As you pray ask God to fill you with His Holy Spirit and manifest a new love in you. Praise and thank Him for giving you that great love for others and setting you free from pride.

References/Homework

Read daily a chapter each of Psalms (an act of worship) and Proverbs (for wisdom).

Galatians 5:16-18	Lust between flesh and Spirit
Proverbs 11:2; 13:10	Pride and wisdom
James 4:6	Strength in humility
Galatians 6:3	Sharing burdens versus pride
Proverbs 20:6	Faithfulness versus pride
1 Corinthians 1:29	No boasting before God
Philippians 2:3	Think of others as better than yourself
1 John 2:16	Pride issuing from wealth and importance
Proverbs 27:2	Let strangers praise thee
Obadiah 3	Pride of heart deceives
1 John 2:16	Lust of the flesh and eyes and pride of life

RECONCILIATION

Victims of broken relationships also have other problems which are intensified as a result of their experience. Bitterness, resentment, anger, frustration and other negative emotions usually aggravate the situation. Often, physical illness follows. However, God is working in all things to reconcile the world to Himself by Jesus Christ (2 Corinthians 5:18; Romans 8:28). The Church has been given the ministry of reconciling parents and children, husbands and wives, labor and management, God and man, and individual and individual.

What Scripture Says

"And all things are of God, who hath reconciled us to himself by Jesus Christ, and hath given to us the ministry of reconciliation; To wit, that God was in Christ, reconciling the world unto himself, not imputing their trespasses unto them; and hath committed unto us the word of reconciliation" (2 Corinthians 5:18, 19).

"And, having made peace through the blood of his cross, by him to reconcile all things unto himself; by him, I say, whether they be things in earth, or things in heaven" (Colossians 1:20).

"Therefore if thou bring thy gift to the altar, and there rememberest that thy brother hath aught against thee; Leave there thy gift before the altar, and go thy way; first be reconciled to thy brother, and then come and offer thy gift" (Matthew 5:23, 24).

"Agree with thine adversary quickly, whiles thou art in the way with him; lest at any time the adversary deliver thee to the judge, and the judge deliver thee to the officer, and thou be cast into prison. Verily I say unto thee, Thou shalt by no means come out thence, till thou hast paid the uttermost farthing" (Matthew 5:25, 26).

"Moreover if thy brother shall trespass against thee, go and tell him his fault between thee and him alone: if he shall hear thee, thou hast gained thy brother. But if he will not hear thee, then take with thee one or two more, that in the mouth of two or three witnesses every word may be established. And if he shall neglect to hear them, tell it unto the church: but if he neglect to hear the church, let him be unto thee as an heathen man and publican. Verily I say unto you, Whatsoever ye shall bind on earth shall be bound in heaven: and whatsoever ye shall loose on earth shall be loosed in heaven. Again I say unto you, That if two of you shall agree on earth as touching any thing that they shall ask, it shall be done for them of my Father which is in heaven" (Matthew 18:15-19).

How to Reconcile Relationships

Reconciliation can be achieved by coming to agreement, first with God and then with your fellowman. Sin separates you from God, allowing Satan to flood your life with tragedy, trauma and destruction. But God's promises are YEA and AMEN. The Spirit of the Lord shall "lift up a standard" against Satan in your behalf when you become a child of God (Isaiah 59). God has put His words of reconciliation in the mouth of His redeemed, the Church (Isaiah 59:20, 21).

Basically, all of your problems are spiritual in nature, so you need the reconciling witness of the Holy Spirit in your life (Matthew 6:33). But you must repent of sins such as bitterness, resentment, fear, and anxiety. They are products of a spiritual desert. God wants you to be saved and to receive the baptism with the Holy Spirit. The Holy Spirit will give you the ability to be reconciled to those with whom you have broken relationships. He can produce love, joy, peace, goodness, kindness, meekness, faithfulness, patience and self-control in you. You will be the kind of person who can be reconciled with anyone.

As You Pray

Release your spouse, parent, child, or whomever to God (Matthew 18:15-19). He loves them as He loves you, and as you pray for them, ask God to give you a great love for them, and to show you how to bless them. Seek the Lord for guidance. Ask Him to reveal any hindrances to reconciliation in your own life. As you pray for rec-

RECONCILIATION

onciliation with God, also pray that all barriers to the restoration of other relationships will be removed.

References/Homework

Hebrews 2   Jesus, the Priest of reconciliation
Romans 12   Practical exhortation
Ephesians 2   All people reconciled to God

Notes

_____

_____

_____

_____

_____

_____

_____

_____

REMARRIAGE

This particular subject remains a very sensitive and difficult issue within the body of Christ. Each case is different, and in every circumstance you should move slowly, pray earnestly, and seek godly counsel.

God's Word does permit remarriage when a spouse dies; however, the Bible discourages it in other cases, except when a person is deserted by an unbeliever or when adultery committed by the other partner causes the marriage to end in divorce.

What Scripture Says

"But if the unbelieving partner (actually) leaves, let him do so; in such (cases the remaining) brother or sister is not morally bound. But God has called us to peace" (1 Corinthians 7:15, Amplified).

"And I say unto you: Whoever dismisses (repudiates, divorces) his wife, except for unchastity, and marries another, commits adultery; and he who marries a divorced woman commits adultery" (Matthew 19:9, Amplified).

"A wife is bound to her husband by the law as long as he lives. If the husband dies, she is free to be married to whom she will, only (provided that he too is) in the Lord" (1 Corinthians 7:39, Amplified).

"My desire is to have you free from all anxiety and distressing care. The unmarried (man) is anxious about the things of the Lord, how he may please the Lord; but the married man is anxious about worldly matters, how he may please his wife. And he is drawn in diverging directions—his interests are divided, and he is distracted (from his devotion to God). And the unmarried woman or girl is concerned and anxious about the matters of the Lord, how to be wholly separated and set apart in body and spirit; but the married woman has her cares (centered) in earthly affairs, how she may please her husband. Now I say this for your own welfare and profit, not to put (a halter of) restraint upon you, but to promote what is seemly and of good order and to secure your undistracted and undivided devotion to the Lord" (1 Corinthians 7:32-35, Amplified).

Counsel Concerning Remarriage

In 1 Corinthians 7:15, it appears that a believer who has been abandoned by an unbeliever is not morally bound to remain married. If so, the believer may remarry only in the Lord.

In Matthew 19:9, Scripture suggests that when fornication has been committed by a party in the marriage, the innocent party may remarry only in the Lord.

In 1 Corinthians 7:39, the Word is very clear that when a spouse dies, the remaining person is free to remarry only in the Lord.

In 1 Corinthians 7:32-35, the Word discourages remarriage for the reasons stated. Ponder these words carefully, for they may protect you from further failures and help you to receive clear direction from the Lord concerning His will for you.

When a marriage has dissolved, for whatever reason—fornication, adultery, or other reason—every effort should be made to restore the relationship. It seems that our primary difficulty as humans is in the area of forgiveness, yet we are exhorted in Scripture to forgive in order to be forgiven! (Matthew 6:14, 15).

In regard to divorces and remarriages that have occurred before becoming a Christian, it seems clear that all such things are part of the old life you have left behind (2 Corinthians 5:17). In other words, if you were married, divorced, and then remarried, and then are born again in the midst of your second marriage, you should not divorce your present spouse to return to the first.

All remarriage plans other than those on the permissive scriptural grounds previously stated must be dealt with as sin and confessed (1 John 1:9). Seek sound biblical counsel from a local pastor or counselor before any final remarriage plans are made.

Once you receive sanction from the Lord concerning your remarriage plans, then you are scripturally bound and accountable to all of God's Word concerning marriage.

As You Pray

In all cases where remarriage is being considered, you should confess your sin and repent of any part you may have had in your previous marriage failure. If there is any guilt, bitterness, or unforgiveness from the previous marriage, pray and ask God to set you free. Pray for God's clear direction in your new life.

References/Homework

Read *The Christian Family,* Larry Christenson.

1 Corinthians 7:2, 8, 9	Let every man have his own wife Let every woman have her own husband
1 Timothy 5:14	Younger widows to marry
1 Corinthians 13	Love in action
Ephesians 5	Duty to spouses
Colossians 3	Duty to spouses
1 Corinthians 7	The marriage bond
1 Peter 3:1-7	Responsibilities of spouses

Notes

_____

_____

_____

_____

_____

_____

_____

_____

_____

REPENTANCE

A famous teacher of the past said that if "your life has no joy in it, and no victory in it, and no happiness in it, I know why. You have not repented." To repent is a critically important, but often neglected, requirement of entering into or restoring a right relationship with God and other persons (Acts 3:19; Luke 15:21). Repentance means you turn from sin and living for yourself, and surrender your life to the lordship of Jesus Christ.

What Scripture Says

"And the times of this ignorance God winked at; but now commandeth all men every where to repent: Because he hath appointed a day, in the which he will judge the world in righteousness by that man whom he hath ordained; whereof he hath given assurance unto all men, in that he hath raised him from the dead" (Acts 17:30, 31).

"I tell you, Nay: but except ye repent, ye shall all likewise perish" (Luke 13:3; note: same condemnation for all).

"Now I rejoice, not that ye were made sorry, but that ye sorrowed to repentance: for ye were made sorry after a godly manner, that ye might receive damage by us in nothing. For godly sorrow worketh repentance to salvation not to be repented of: but the sorrow of the world worketh death" (2 Corinthians 7:9, 10).

"The Lord is not slack concerning his promise, as some men count slackness; but is longsuffering to us-ward, not willing that any should perish, but that all should come to repentance" (2 Peter 3:9).

"I say unto you, that likewise joy shall be in heaven over one sinner that repenteth, more than over ninety and nine just persons, which need no repentance" (Luke 15:7).

REPENTANCE

Sinful Nature Requires Repentance

We are all born with a sinful nature of self-consciousness. With such a nature we cannot enter into righteous, acceptable fellowship with God and our fellowman.

Every problem you will ever face in life can be traced to your natural, sinful state of being. But God works through everything that happens in your life to draw you to Jesus so that you might repent and be saved (John 6:44, 45; 14:6; Romans 8:28).

God said that you must be born again of the Spirit of God (John 3:3, 5). This means you turn your life over to Jesus as Savior and Lord, in repentance and faith that He will forgive and cleanse you from all sin (Romans 3:23; 10:13; 1 John 1:8, 9; John 1:12).

To walk in the righteousness of God, the Bible says that your fleshliness with its lusts and affections must be put under subjection. Otherwise you will be controlled by it (Romans 6:6; 13:14; Galatians 5:16).

Yielding to the appetites of the flesh and being controlled by the fickle dictates of your natural thinking leads to "works of the flesh" that are physically, emotionally and spiritually destructive. These include immorality, impurity, sensuality, idolatry, outbursts of anger, disputes, dissensions, factions, envying, drunkenness, carousing, etc. Such works of the flesh, if not repented of, result in spiritual death (Galatians 5:19-21; James 1:15).

Any attitude or action which is not born of faith, is sin (Romans 14:23; 1 John 5:17; James 4:17). Many sins do not seem to be sin, but they are not faith-filled responses to our circumstances and relationships. These include anxiety, worry, fear, suicide, bitterness, resentment, and many occult practices such as fortune-telling, horoscopy, numerology, astrology, and others. Many sicknesses result from sinful attitudes, such as arthritis, which is sometimes a result of fear, anxiety, or bitterness and resentment (1 Corinthians 2:28-30). You must take seriously the fact that God is holy and righteous and can't look upon sin, and that "the wages of sin is death" (Romans 6:23).

When your old life is exchanged for a new nature in Christ, through repentance and faith in Him, you need continuous spiritual nourishment. Therefore, you need to be in a church where you can grow spiritually. Read the Bible daily during a quiet time. Pray ceaselessly.

As You Pray

Repent of self-conscious lusts, pride and of desiring to have your own way. Ask God to forgive and cleanse you for your unrighteous way of life. Surrender completely to Him, ask Him to be the Lord of your life, and commit yourself totally to Him. Thank and praise God for convicting you of sin, of judgment, and of His righteousness.

References/Homework

Read *Repentance,* Basilea Schlink.

Psalm 51	Example of true repentance—David
Exodus 9:27-35	Example of insincere repentance

Sinful nature and what to do about it:

Romans 5:12-19	Sin and death
1 John 3:4	Sin is against God
James 4:17	Knowledge and sin
Matthew 15:18-20	Evil words and thoughts defile
Romans 3:23	All have sinned
1 John 1:8, 10	Sin confessed is forgiven

Notes

_____

_____

_____

_____

_____

_____

_____

SALVATION (ADULTS)

Sin is the cause of almost every problem you will ever face in life. But there is a way to have victory over sin: forgiveness in Jesus Christ. To experience this, you must be born again. It is God's greatest desire for you. Even if you think you have all your immediate problems solved, what good will it do you in the long run if you lose your own soul?

The Bible teaches that salvation, which consists of being born again and having your sins forgiven, is necessary in order to see the Kingdom of God (John 3:3), to receive eternal life and the indwelling Holy Spirit, and to become a child of God and joint heir with Christ. You receive salvation by faith in the death and resurrection of Christ for the atonement of your sins. Salvation includes a turning from sin and self-centered life (repentance) and a turning over of the direction of your life completely to Jesus (lordship of Christ). Salvation is also totally by God's grace: He elects, predestines, calls, justifies, sanctifies and glorifies every true believer (Romans 8:29, 30; Ephesians 2:8, 9).

What Scripture Says

"Jesus answered and said unto him, Verily, verily, I say unto thee, except a man be born again, he cannot see the kingdom of God" (John 3:3).

"For all have sinned, and come short of the glory of God" (Romans 3:23).

"For whosoever shall call upon the name of the Lord shall be saved" (Romans 10:13).

"But as many as received him, to them gave he power to become the sons of God, even to them that believe on his name" (John 1:12).

"If we confess our sins, he is faithful and just to forgive us our sins, and to cleanse us from all unrighteousness" (1 John 1:9).

SALVATION (ADULTS)

God's Plan of Salvation

If you have not yet trusted Christ as Lord and Savior, that is your foremost need. Salvation is not earned. It is by grace through faith (Ephesians 2:8, 9). Pray according to the above Scripture. Trust God for the results.

After praying, believe that God has heard and in His faithfulness has saved you. Contact a local Bible-believing church for water baptism, church fellowship, Bible study and spiritual growth.

Upon becoming a Christian you are a candidate for the baptism with the Holy Spirit. A local Spirit-filled ministry will be happy to help you understand the baptism and will pray with you to receive it.

As You Pray

Call on Jesus, confess your sins, and receive Him as Savior and Lord. He knows your heart and will answer your prayer.

If you wish, you can pray in this manner: "Jesus, forgive me of my sin. I take You at Your Word that You forgive those who ask. Be my Lord, as You are my Savior. I give myself to You. I'm Yours. Thank You for being faithful and saving me. I've asked and believe that You have saved me. Amen."

References/Homework

Other Scripture:

Romans 6:23	A gift
Ephesians 2:8, 9	A gift
2 Timothy 1:9	A gift
Matthew 3:1, 2	By repentance and confession
Matthew 10:32, 33	By repentance and confession
Luke 15:10	By repentance and confession
Acts 3:19	By repentance and confession
Acts 2:38, 39	By repentance and confession
Romans 2:4	By repentance and confession
Romans 10:9, 10	By repentance and confession
2 Peter 3:9	By repentance and confession

1 John 1:9	By repentance and confession
Mark 13:13	Assurance of salvation
John 3:16	Assurance of salvation
John 5:24	Assurance of salvation
John 10:27, 28	Assurance of salvation
Romans 10:13	Assurance of salvation
1 Peter 1:3-5	Assurance of salvation
1 John 2:25	Assurance of salvation
1 John 5:13	Assurance of salvation
Revelation 3:20, 21	Assurance of salvation

Notes

_____

_____

_____

_____

_____

_____

_____

_____

_____

SALVATION (CHILD)

Do you know Jesus Christ as your Savior? Do you want to? The Bible says that if you ask Jesus to save you, He will (Romans 10:13). Jesus came into the world to give us a new, eternal life that will never end (John 3:16). And He came to give us a good life here on earth (John 10:10). Even though we will still have problems sometimes, He will always be with us and meet our needs.

What Scripture Says

Read these Bible verses. They tell of God's plan for you to be saved. If a friend or your brother, sister or parents are with you, you can read them together.

"For God so loved the world, that he gave his only begotten Son, that whosoever believeth in him should not perish, but have everlasting life" (John 3:16).

"For whosoever shall call upon the name of the Lord shall be saved" (Romans 10:13).

"If we say that we have no sin, we deceive ourselves, and the truth is not in us. If we confess our sins, he is faithful and just to forgive us our sins, and to cleanse us from all unrighteousness" (1 John 1:8, 9).

"But as many as received him, to them gave he power to become the sons of God, even to them that believe on his name" (John 1:12).

"Behold, I stand at the door, and knock: If any man hear my voice, and open the door, I will come in to him, and will sup with him, and he with me" (Revelation 3:20).

If you are not sure what the verses mean, ask someone who is already a Christian to help you understand. Your Sunday school teacher or church pastor will be glad to help.

206

SALVATION (CHILD)

As You Pray

You may pray in your own words and ask Jesus to forgive you of your sin and come into your heart. Thank Jesus for answering your prayer.

Read the verses again. Can you see that God's Word says that you are saved? You have done what God said to do to be saved. Let the Holy Spirit make it real to you.

What Next?

Be obedient to God's Word. Read the Bible every day. Start with the book of John in the New Testament. Then read Acts, Matthew, Luke, Romans, and other books in the Bible. The church you go to will help you decide what to read next.

When you commit sin, confess it to the Lord immediately. Ask His forgiveness. He knows your heart and promises to forgive.

Memorize Bible verses that help you, such as those about salvation.

Talk to God in prayer. Find a quiet time each day to read your Bible and pray.

Meet with Christian friends who also wish to live for Jesus.

Tell others about Jesus and what happened to you. You might tell your family, Sunday school teacher, pastor, friends, etc.

Attend church. Go to a church where there are other Christians who love and help one another.

Our Prayer for You

We pray for you and know that you are safe in the Lord. We thank God that He has forgiven your sin and that you have received Jesus as Savior. We ask Jesus to fill you with the Holy Spirit and love and joy and peace forever.

References/Homework

Write down the chapters and verses above and memorize them. If you don't write yet, ask someone to help you to learn them.

SALVATION (CHILD)

Reading for parents and others who wish to minister to children:

Your Child, Anna B. Mow (Grand Rapids, Michigan: Zondervan Publishing House, 1963); *How to Raise Your Children for Christ,* Andrew Murray (Bethany Fellowship); *Teaching Your Child About God,* Claudia Royal (Revell, 1969).

Reading for children:

"Steps in Growing"—Child Evangelism Fellowship tract (from CBN).

Arch Books (Christian Publications); *Read for Children* (A free monthly publication for children and young people. Address P.O. Box 1017, Arcadia, Florida 33821); *Caterpillar Books* (Christian Publications); *Good News Bible* (American Bible Society); *The Living Bible* (Tyndale).

Notes

SEXUAL SINS

Sexual sins include:

Immorality—moral behavior contrary to God's standards.

Perversion—turning from the true and/or proper purpose of sexual intercourse; misusing or abusing it, such as in homosexuality, sadism, masochism and transvestism.

Adultery—sexual intercourse with a person other than your spouse.

Fornication—illicit sexual intercourse when you aren't married.

Sexual sins are committed because of lust (1 John 2:16; Galatians 5:19-21). When you allow improper sexual drives to control you as a Christian, an inner tension will result in your mind, emotions and will. You will want to be spiritual, but find yourself being a slave to sensuality. The result is double-mindedness (James 1:8), leading to a reprobate mind (Romans 1:28).

What Scripture Says

"And likewise also the men, leaving the natural use of the woman, burned in their lust one toward another; men with men working that which is unseemly, and receiving in themselves that recompense of their error which was meet. And even as they did not like to retain God in their knowledge, God gave them over to a reprobate mind, to do those things which are not convenient" (Romans 1:27, 28).

"Marriage is honorable in all, and the bed undefiled: but whore-mongers and adulterers God will judge" (Hebrews 13:4).

"Know ye not that the unrighteous shall not inherit the kingdom of God? Be not deceived: neither fornicators, nor idolaters, nor adulterers, nor effeminate, nor abusers of themselves with mankind, nor thieves, nor covetous, nor drunkards, nor revilers, nor extortioners, shall inherit the kingdom of God" (1 Corinthians 6:9, 10).

SEXUAL SINS

"But fornication, and all uncleanness, or covetousness, let it not be once named among you, as becometh saints" (Ephesians 5:3).

Your Spiritual Health Is Affected

You may break God's laws, but by your disobedience you will wreck your life and the lives of many others. It is impossible to involve yourself in sexual sin without damaging your spiritual nature and that of your partner, your families, friends, etc. You may try to "tune out" the spiritual aspects involved, but will succeed only in deadening your conscience to spiritual truth. You will then be guilty of tampering with your inner spiritual core and that of your partner and others. The scars from this kind of involvement are ugly, deep, and long-lasting. God cares too much for you and all of His children to leave such tampering and spiritual abuse unpunished.

How to Be Free

To be free from sexual lusts, you must repent. Just as in the past you have allowed lust to control your flesh, you must now yield to God as the Holy Spirit convicts you of your sin. God will forgive you and cleanse you physically, emotionally and spiritually as you call on Him in repentance and faith. He will save you from sin's consequences and put His nature within you (Romans 3:23; 6:23; 1 John 1:8, 9; Romans 10:13; John 1:12).

To overcome temptations, follow God's plan for resisting them. Minister to God with sacrifices of praise (Hebrews 13:15), until you are filled with the peace and joy of the Lord (Isaiah 26:3). That is when your praise has become acceptable to God and He has ministered release from the temptation.

Finally, you need the ability to live the righteous, holy, abundant life that God has for you as you are filled with His love. The baptism with the Holy Spirit enables you to become more like Christ: able to overcome sin, to pray effectively and to help other people who need to be saved and know God in His fullness. As you grow in the Lord, you need to become part of a vibrant, Spirit-filled church. Follow a planned way of studying the Bible daily. Pray constantly and fellowship with other like-minded Christians. If you still experience temptations, you need the help of a Spirit-filled minister, counselor and/or other prayer partners.

As You Pray

Thank and praise God for forgiving, cleansing and strengthening you to stand fast in His liberty. Pray for others who were involved in your sins, that they, too, will be delivered from sexual lusts and sins.

References/Homework

Acts 15:20; 1 Corinthians 5:1; 6:13-18; 7:2; 1 Thessalonians 4:3	Fornication
Proverbs 2:16-19; 6:20; 7:27; 9:13-18	Adultery
Genesis 38:1-10; Romans 1:18-32	Perversion

Study these Scripture injunctions and promises. Above all, minister praises (honor and respect) to God until He delivers you. Each time you face temptation, continuously praise Him, enthroning Him in your thoughts instead of allowing the temptations to gain control. The following verses will show you how to gain victory through praise:

1 Thessalonians 5:18; Ephesians 5:20	Give thanks in and for everything
Romans 8:28	Reason for thanks
Hebrews 13:15	Sacrifice of praise
Psalm 22:3	Enthrone God
Isaiah 26:3	God gives peace

Notes

_____

_____

_____

_____

SMOKING

Are you enslaved by the desire to smoke? Are you unable to stop smoking and remain free of the habit?

The Bible says that it is not what goes into a person that defiles him, but what comes out of his mouth. In other words, you can condemn yourself not with food or tobacco but by what you say, confess, testify to verbally, teach, or preach.

However, when you smoke you are in bondage. You may find it almost impossible to quit even though it is damaging your body, God's temple of the Holy Spirit. Furthermore, smoking hurts your Christian witness because it is offensive to others (1 Corinthians 8:7-13).

What Scripture Says

"What? know ye not that your body is the temple of the Holy Ghost which is in you, which ye have of God, and ye are not your own? For ye are bought with a price: therefore glorify God in your body, and in your spirit, which are God's" (1 Corinthians 6:19, 20).

"While they promise them liberty, they themselves are the servants of corruption: for of whom a man is overcome, of the same is he brought in bondage" (2 Peter 2:19).

"Let not sin therefore reign in your mortal body, that ye should obey it in the lusts thereof" (Romans 6:12).

"Let every one of us please his neighbour for his good to edification. For even Christ pleased not himself; but, as it is written, The reproaches of them that reproached thee fell on me" (Romans 15:2, 3).

How to Be Free

First, you need to turn your life over to God, to be born again. As you call upon the Lord, repent of having yielded your body to the unclean, destructive foulness of smoking (whether tobacco, marijuana, or another substance).

To receive power to resist the temptation to smoke, ask God to baptize you with the Holy Spirit. Ask Him to deliver you from the desire to smoke, both physical and mental. And thank Him for doing it. Jesus knows your need to be clean and free of this damaging habit. He will answer while you are praying.

If temptation returns, tell yourself, "I am not going to smoke right now." Then stop thinking about whether to smoke or not. Occupy your mind with God and His Word and worshiping Him. Honor Him, not your habit. Remember that what you honor in your life, what you focus your attention on, crave and desire, will be your paymaster. If you honor your habit, it will pay off in ill health, alienation in your close relationships with others, and even early death.

Praise God each time you want to smoke. The greater the temptation, the more you should praise Him. "Sacrifice" praise until you are joyfully worshiping the Lord in praise, thanksgiving, and even with spirited song. When the sacrifice of praise is acceptable to God, you will know it. The temptation will be gone (Hebrews 13:15; Psalm 22:3; Isaiah 26:3).

God can instantly deliver you from the desire to smoke, psychologically and physically. Yet it does not always happen this way. Like many people, you may have to exercise your willpower and mean business with yourself and God before you are free. If you are having problems quitting, you should ask someone to pray for you and with you. Undoubtedly, there are others in your church who have successfully "kicked the habit." Seek their help and prayers. You can be free. Settle for nothing less. Ask God to produce the fruit of the Spirit, willpower (self-control).

As You Pray

Thank and praise God who is (right now) delivering you from the desire to smoke.

Ask for an anointing with the Holy Spirit. As you do, begin to praise God for it. Expect Him to fill you with the Holy Spirit and willpower.

Thank God for cleansing and forgiving you. He honors those who honor Him. Determine to be free.

It often takes three days to two weeks to be free from psychological and physical cravings. Don't despair. Be determined. God is faithful. He will honor your determination.

References/Homework

1 John 5:4, 5	Victory in Christ
Philippians 4:13	Victory in Christ
1 John 4:4	Victory in Christ
1 Corinthians 10:13	God is faithful
Psalm 22:3	Enthrone Him in praise
Hebrews 13:15	Sacrifice praise to God

Notes

_____

_____

_____

_____

_____

_____

_____

_____

_____

SUBMISSION

The Bible commands us to submit ourselves to God, resisting Satan who will flee from us (James 4:7). From that point, other relationships can be established in proper perspective.

If you are not able to take advice or accept another person as he is without demanding that he change, you may be in rebellion against God. Such rebellion is reflected in relations between husbands and wives, employees and employers, and children and parents. Both Christians and non-Christians find themselves rebellious toward God and toward other people.

What Scripture Says

"From whence come wars and fightings among you? come they not hence, even of your lusts that war in your members? . . . Submit yourselves therefore to God. Resist the devil, and he will flee from you" (James 4:1, 7).

"Likewise, ye younger, submit yourselves unto the elder. Yea, all of you be subject one to another, and be clothed with humility: for God resisteth the proud, and giveth grace to the humble. Humble yourselves therefore under the mighty hand of God, that he may exalt you in due time" (1 Peter 5:5, 6).

"Nevertheless let every one of you in particular so love his wife even as himself; and the wife see that she reverence her husband" (Ephesians 5:33).

"Submitting yourselves one to another in the fear of God. Wives, submit yourselves unto your own husbands, as unto the Lord. For the husband is the head of the wife, even as Christ is the head of the church: and he is the saviour of the body" (Ephesians 5:21-23).

"Likewise, ye wives, be in subjection to your own husbands; that, if any obey not the word, they also may without the word be won by the conversation of the wives; While they behold your chaste conversation coupled with fear. Whose adorning, let it not be that outward adorning of plaiting the hair, and of wearing of gold, or of putting on of apparel; But let it be the hidden man of the heart, in that which is not corruptible, even the ornament of a meek and quiet spirit, which is in the sight of God of great price" (1 Peter 3:1-4).

"Servants, be obedient to them that are your masters according to the flesh, with fear and trembling, in singleness of heart, as unto Christ; Not with eye-service, as menpleasers; but as the servants of Christ, doing the will of God from the heart; With good will doing service, as to the Lord, and not to men: Knowing that whatsoever good thing any man doeth, the same shall he receive of the Lord, whether he be bond or free. And, ye masters, do the same things unto them, forbearing threatening: knowing that your Master also is in heaven; neither is there respect of persons with Him" (Ephesians 6:5-9).

"Children, obey your parents in the Lord: for this is right. Honour thy father and mother; which is the first commandment with promise; That it may be well with thee, and thou mayest live long on the earth. And, ye fathers, provoke not your children to wrath: but bring them up in the nurture and admonition of the Lord" (Ephesians 6:1-4).

The Reward of Submission

When the divine order of submission is followed, relationships improve and are set right. Rebellion ceases and harmony follows. You can learn God's will for your life and have your needs met as fellow Christians pray and seek God's counsel for you (James 5:14-16). You then judge their counsel, since you are still responsible for your actions before God.

The Bible teaches that you must submit yourself to God unreservedly. It also says you should be in submission to those in authority over you, such as parents, employers, church leaders and the government (Deuteronomy 11:27; Jeremiah 42:6; Ephesians 6:1; Colossians 3:20, 22; 2 Thessalonians 3:14; Hebrews 13:17.)

Obviously, there is a point beyond which you cannot go in submitting to human beings and man-made laws. Anything or anyone making demands that are clearly against God's Word should not be obeyed (Acts 5:29); nor should you feel compelled to those who would set themselves up to be spiritual dictators, such as did many of the Pharisees of Jesus' days on earth (Matthew 23). Everything must be judged by the Scriptures, but be aware of "crafty teachers" who are deceived themselves and either knowingly or unknowingly would deceive you (2 Peter 3:17; Jude 4, 8, 10, 16, 18, 19).

Learn to submit to God and to others in authority. But search the Scriptures and memorize passages daily in order to wisely judge their counsel. Act upon the Scriptures, letting them affect your daily life.

Prayer, praise and submission to God show honor and respect to Him. If you show God honor and respect, you will receive honor and respect from Him. It is the same with men honoring men. As you humble (submit) yourself and ask for wise counsel and help, men will honor you and your requests of them.

As You Pray

Praise and thank God, asking Him to reveal any area of pride in your life. Thank Him for His forgiveness as you repent of pride. Ask God for the fruit of the Spirit "meekness" which basically means to be humbly submissive to God. The meek shall inherit the earth (Matthew 5:5) because they can be entrusted with it as they are submissive to God.

References/Homework

Matthew 6:10; 26:39	Jesus was in submission to God
Luke 1:38	Jesus' mother submitted herself to God
Romans 12	Especially verse 10, prefer one another
Romans 6:13	Submit your body to God
James 5:14-16	Submit to prayers of others
Galatians 5:22, 23	Fruit of the Spirit

SUBMISSION
(Shepherdship)

The submission (shepherdship) movement is a covenant relationship where an elder or "shepherd" is submitted to in all matters, religious or otherwise. The movement, also referred to as "discipleship," began in the United States in the mid-1970s.

The movement can be described as a religious dictatorship. Elders are often self-appointed and gather around them those who will follow their teachings and accept their authority. An elder often submits to the authority of another elder in a chain of command similar to other hierarchies. Total discipline is usually imposed over biblical interpretation, self-will, desire, actions, etc., with self and family under the imposed will of the elder. The tithes and offerings are often given to the elder who decides how to use them. Spiritual and mental bondage often result from being under a shepherdship covenant relationship.

What Scripture Says

"And when he putteth forth his own sheep, he goeth before them, and the sheep follow him: for they know his voice. . . . And a stranger will they not follow, but will flee from him: for they know not the voice of strangers . . . my sheep hear my voice, and I know them and they follow me" (John 10:4, 5, 27).

"For, brethren, ye have been called unto liberty; only use not liberty for an occasion to the flesh, but by love serve one another" (Galatians 5:13).

"And ye shall know the truth, and the truth shall make you free" (John 8:32).

"Because the creature itself also shall be delivered from the bondage of corruption into the glorious liberty of the children of God" (Romans 8:21).

218

"For there is one God, and one mediator between God and men, the man Christ Jesus" (1 Timothy 2:5).

"And he said unto them, The kings of the Gentiles exercise lordship over them; and they that exercise authority upon them are called benefactors. But ye shall not be so: but he that is greatest among you, let him be as the younger; and he that is chief, as he that doth serve" (Luke 22:25, 26).

"Howbeit when he, the Spirit of truth, is come, he will guide you into all truth: for he shall not speak of himself; but whatsoever he shall hear, that shall he speak: and he will shew you things to come" (John 16:13).

Explanation and Counsel

There are positive aspects of the covenant relationship movement: the Bible is taught; it is full-gospel oriented; many people are ministered to by the elders and others in the fellowship; and it emphasizes that every Christian should be diligently taught (discipled) and should have someone close at hand when help is needed.

The Bible does say that we should submit ourselves one to another and in honor prefer one another (Romans 12:10). We also speak of having a spiritual covering such as the pastor of our church. But after asking someone in whom we have confidence to pray for us and give us counsel, we must still make our own decisions. We cannot excuse a bad decision by telling God that "my shepherd made me do it" (Romans 14:12; Mark 10:42-45).

Allow no one to tell you how to live your life, whom you shall marry, that you should divorce your spouse, where to work, whether to visit your relatives, etc. Remember that God does not contradict Himself, nor is He the author of confusion (1 Corinthians 14:33).

There is no harm in seeking wise counsel, which would include prayer and Scripture teachings. However, this is not the same as being told what to do and given no alternative other than being cast out of the fellowship and put under condemnation for disobeying the shepherd.

Jesus was obedient to the Father. He did the works and spoke the words of the Father (John 14:10). The Holy Spirit reveals Jesus' counsel to the believer (John 16:13). The individual believer is to go directly to God the Father because of his own position in Christ. Christ did away with the barrier (the curtain) separating us from God's "holy of holies" when He died on the cross. A Christian still prays in intercession for others, but only Jesus is the mediator between God and man. The biblical teaching of "the priesthood of the believer" removes the need for any other "go-between" between a Christian and God, except as you may pray in intercession for another. Study the above passages. Also see Revelation 1:6. Every man is still held responsible for his own behavior.

Although there is no other mediator than Jesus (1 Timothy 2:5), there are prophets, teachers, pastors, evangelists and apostles for the perfecting of the saints, the work of the ministry and edification of the body of Christ (cf. Ephesians 4:11, 12). These ministers do have authority in the Holy Spirit, but they are not spiritual dictators.

There have always been religious bodies which have been dominated by one person, and others which believe that they alone have God's Word. They have often started well, but their end has been corruption and spiritual bondage. The Bible says that in the mouth of two or three witnesses, a truth is established (2 Corinthians 13:1; Deuteronomy 17:6; Matthew 18:16). To avoid collusion of witnesses, look for independent confirmations of a "word from God." Then follow what you believe God is saying, and not what someone else says He is saying.

Be careful not to be brought under bondage to a hierarchical system or to the leader of such a system. True shepherds are those who, in every instance, give their "all" (lives) for the sheep of their pasture. Look for the shepherd (pastor) or elder who follows Jesus' example to serve, not to be served (Mark 10:45). The Holy Spirit produces self-control, not control by others (Galatians 5:22, 23).

Finally, consider what you would do if an elder were not present when needed. You must hear God's voice. Jesus said, "My sheep hear my voice." No other mediator is needed. The Lord (Jesus) must be your shepherd. No other shepherd must be your Lord.

SUBMISSION (SHEPHERDSHIP)

As You Pray

Pray in agreement with God's Word that the Holy Spirit will guide you into all truth (John 14:26; 16:13). Pray that any bondage will be broken and that only a great love, even for the shepherdship teachers and elders, will prevail. Pray to forgive any error of the flesh and ignorance. Pray for all to be in unity in the Spirit.

References/Homework

Read *Discipleship: The Jesus View,* Bill Ligon with Robert Paul Lamb.

2 Corinthians 3:17	Spirit gives freedom
Galatians 2:4	Not in bondage to others
Romans 6:16	You are slaves to the master you obey
2 Peter 2:1a, 2a, 19	False teachings bring enslavement to false teachers
Revelation 19:20	Ultimate defeat of the false prophet
Psalm 23	True Shepherd

Notes

_____

_____

_____

_____

_____

_____

_____

_____

_____

SUICIDE

The desire or decision to kill yourself is often a result of depression. You may be depressed because of health problems, pain, or the inability to face frustrations in life. You may also feel self-pity, guilt, anxiety, and frustration as a result of your natural, sinful condition of self-consciousness.

Or it may be that you have an irrational desire to "end it all" and destroy yourself as a result of irresponsible behavior. You may be ensnared by demon possession or obsession. Involvement in cultish teaching or mob influence can also result in a suicide psychology.

If you have suicidal tendencies, you may feel you have run out of hope, have been let down by those you depended on, or have nothing left to live for. Yet, as a Christian, your hope and strength to carry on are in the Lord (Psalm 42:11). The heavens may seem as brass, and your prayers, even when accompanied by tears, may seem useless. But with faith in God, you can have deliverance, healing and "hope springing eternal."

What Scripture Says

"But he saveth the poor from the sword, from their mouth, and from the hand of the mighty" (Job 5:15).

"I will bless the Lord at all times: his praise shall continually be in my mouth. . . . The angel of the Lord encampeth round about them that fear him, and delivereth them" (Psalm 34:1, 7).

"He that dwelleth in the secret place of the most High shall abide under the shadow of the Almighty. . . . For he shall give his angels charge over thee, to keep thee in all thy ways. They shall bear thee up in their hands, lest thou dash thy foot against a stone. . . . I will deliver him, and honour him. With long life will I satisfy him and shew him my salvation" (Psalm 91:1, 11-12, 15-16).

"The thief cometh not, but for to steal, and to kill, and to destroy:

222

I am come that they might have life, and that they might have it more abundantly" (John 10:10).

What to Do

If you have had thoughts of suicide, it is time to closely examine your life and find out where you are "coming from." You must understand the cause of the problem in order to find God's answers for you.

Ask yourself "what" questions: What is wrong physically? What is wrong emotionally? And, most importantly, what is wrong spiritually? Do not minimize your answers to these questions. Be honest with yourself, with others and with God. It is important to define for yourself exactly what you are feeling and experiencing. Evaluate your situation seriously. You are so important and so loved by God that He has provided counselors and ministers who are anointed by the Holy Spirit to help you. They will be able to help or refer you to someone who can.

Problems are easier to deal with individually. It is like the story of the parrot who could say only one phrase. As he was being stung by a nest full of hornets, he spoke the only words he knew: "One at a time, please." That is how you can handle YOUR problems— one at a time. Ask yourself specific "what" questions: What is my main problem? What are problems within that problem?

As you try to determine where you are spiritually, your first question should be, "Have I been born again of the Spirit of God?" (John 3:3-8, 16). You can have new life in Christ. No matter how bad your sins, God loves you enough to have sent Jesus just so you can be saved from the consequences of life without Him.

God said that every need you have will be supplied after you have been born into His kingdom and begin a new life with Christ (Matthew 6:25-34). When you receive Jesus into your life, you become an "authorized child" of God (John 1:12).

Power and Help Available

Everyone needs the ability to live a life filled with purpose and happiness. You may not have found that ability yet, even if you are already a born-again Christian. You need the baptism with the Holy

SUICIDE

Spirit who gives the dynamic ability to have an abundant life, no matter what your circumstances (John 10:10; 14:12-17; 16:13-15; Acts 1:8). The Holy Spirit will work within you to produce a new nature with the character traits of: love, joy, peace, goodness, kindness, meekness, faithfulness, patience and self-control (Galatians 5:22, 23). With these character traits and with God's armor about you (Ephesians 6:10-18), you can become a new person, able in the Lord to control your circumstances with "room to spare," whatever the problems.

If you suspect that you are being "attacked by demonic spirits" (Ephesians 6:12, 13), do not hesitate to contact our Nationwide Counseling Number, (800) 446-0700. If there is a local ministry in which you have confidence, contact them and explain your experiences and suspicions as you ask for their help. Suspect demonic activity if you are: hearing voices, having compulsive suicidal thoughts that you can't get out of your mind, experiencing thoughts of harming other people, having fear that you can't overcome, having overwhelming anxieties, noticing that people react to you strangely or suspiciously, or experiencing other abnormal feelings. Even some physical problems may be caused by demonic spirits.

If you have been involved with occult activities such as fortune-telling, black or white magic, horoscope reading, numerology, witchcraft, seances, so-called "spiritual" readings, and occult games such as the ouija board, Dungeons and Dragons, etc., you should expect demonic depression from Satan, especially if you are having thoughts of suicide. You may have become innocently involved with the occult while seeking meaning for your life. But no matter why you did, repent and ask God's forgiveness for being involved. The occult is from Satan and is an abomination to God (Deuteronomy 18:10-13).

If physical or emotional problems are causing you to think of suicide, first ask God to reveal to you anything in your life that prevents Him from healing you. Contact a local Spirit-filled minister for prayer and counseling with someone who has received the baptism with the Holy Spirit and can minister to you through the gifts of the Holy Spirit. These gifts are the word of knowledge, the word of wisdom, prophecy, healing and working of miracles (1 Corinthians 12:8-10).

God has established His Church. He staffs it with people who are gifted by the Holy Spirit to help you grow, prosper, overcome life's difficulties and Satan's wiles and minister to your needs in all circumstances (Ephesians 4:7-11). Look for a strong, Holy Spirit-led church near you and become involved in it for your spiritual growth and other needs. You may also have Christian friends who can refer you to a vibrant, Bible-teaching church.

As You Pray

Praise and thank God for His concern and love for you. Even though Satan may be trying to destroy you, God will send angels to minister to you (Hebrews 1:7, 14). As you minister praise to Him in honor and respect, He will show honor and respect to you (1 Samuel 2:30b). Surrender all your burdens to Him and thank Him for working all the circumstances in your life for your good (Romans 8:28).

References/Homework

Psalm 40; 42; 43	Hope
Psalm 51	David's prayer for God's mercy
Romans 8:1-13; Isaiah 1:18; Ephesians 2:8, 9	Assurance of grace
Philippians 4:6-8	Thinking on godly things to renew one's mind
Galatians 5:22, 23	Fruit of the Spirit
Psalm 73	Heart's cry of the psalmist and assurance of deliverance in confession and faith in God
Philippians 4:19	God will supply
Matthew 6:25-33	Seek God first—He will supply all needs
Hebrews 7:25	Assurance of salvation
Matthew 7:7-11	Ask, seek and knock to receive from God
John 14	The Holy Spirit promised
John 15	Source of a fruitful life
John 16:7-15	Working of the Holy Spirit

SUICIDE

Acquire a daily devotional Bible reading guide and follow it in a "quiet time" as you pray each day. Also, begin reading daily at least one chapter of Psalms and one chapter of Proverbs for guidance and aid in worship and in gaining wisdom for your life. To read the entire Bible, begin with the Gospel according to John in the New Testament. Then starting at the first book of the Old and New Testaments, read one chapter of each, continuing until you complete the Bible.

Notes

_____

_____

_____

_____

_____

_____

_____

_____

_____

TEMPTATION

To face a temptation to sin is to struggle with an almost overwhelming desire to misuse or abuse what God had intended for your good and appropriate use.

The Christian can turn temptation into a blessing. Temptation shows you your impurities (sinfulness), much like the flux used by a metallurgist causes impurities to rise to the surface of molten metal so that they can be removed. The areas of life through which Satan seeks to destroy you are revealed to you through temptation. Confess your sinfulness and claim God's promise that forgiveness and cleansing follow repentance (1 John 1:9).

What Scripture Says

"There hath no temptation taken you but such as is common to man: but God is faithful, who will not suffer you to be tempted above that ye are able; but will with the temptation also make a way to escape, that ye may be able to bear it" (1 Corinthians 10:13).

"My brethren, count it all joy when ye fall into divers temptations; Knowing this, that the trying of your faith worketh patience. . . . Blessed is the man that endureth temptation: for when he is tried, he shall receive the crown of life, which the Lord hath promised to them that love him" (James 1:2, 3, 12).

"And we know that all things work together for good to them that love God, to them who are the called according to his purpose" (Romans 8:28).

"In every thing give thanks: for this is the will of God in Christ Jesus concerning you" (1 Thessalonians 5:18).

"But thou art holy, O thou that inhabitest the praises of Israel" (Psalm 22:3).

"By him therefore let us offer the sacrifice of praise to God con-

tinually, that is, the fruit of our lips, giving thanks to his name"
(Hebrews 13:15).

How to Overcome Temptation

Your first need is, as always, to be born again and to receive the
baptism with the Holy Spirit. As you become a Christian, you also
need the ability to live an overcoming life. The Holy Spirit will become
your counselor and your strength to resist temptations. He will convict you of what is right and wrong (John 16:7-11).

You can be just as "chained" to sin by trying not to commit it as
you are when you commit it.

Temptation serves to "chain" you to your sinfulness, even though
it is not yielded to. That is because your focus of attention (pre-
eminence) is given over to the temptation, and when you "sow to
the flesh, you will reap corruption" (Galatians 6:7, 8). When you
occupy your mind with sinfulness, you are paid the wages of sin
(Romans 6:23).

The way to overcome temptation is to change your pre-eminence
from sinfulness to God. For example, you need peace and freedom
from the temptation. If you keep your focus of attention on God,
perfect peace is given (Isaiah 26:3). It is a matter of ministering to
God rather than to your flesh. To minister to God, offer sacrifices
of praise to Him continually until peace over the temptation comes
(Hebrews 13:15). When peace and victory come and you are able to
joyfully praise God, you will know that your sacrifices of praise have
been acceptable to Him.

Pray that God will give you the fruit of the Spirit, that you will not
be controlled by your fleshly and intellectual lusts or by pride. You
especially need the fruit of the Spirit meekness (submissiveness to
God) and temperance (self-control), with which you can control temptation rather than being overwhelmed by it (Galatians 5:19-23; 1 John
2:16).

As you think in your heart, so are you. What you read determines
what you think. Therefore, you should carefully evaluate and replace
harmful reading with wholesome material. A Spirit-filled fellowship
of like-minded Christians will help you redefine your life and provide

spiritual activities wherein you are thinking of moral, rather than immoral, things.

As You Pray

Thank and praise God for every temptation (Ephesians 5:20) and for the victory over it. Thank Him for revealing your sinfulness to you and for showing you the way to overcome it as He promised.

References/Homework

Examples of those who resisted and overcame temptation:

Genesis 14:23	Abraham
2 Kings 5:16	Elisha
Job 2:9, 10	Job
Jeremiah 35:5, 6	Refusing wine
Daniel 1:8	Refusing wine
Proverbs 31:4, 5	Refusing wine
Luke 4:5-8	Refusing worldly honor
Acts 8:20	Refusing worldly honor
Revelation 2:7; 12:11	Overcoming
John 16:33	Overcoming

Notes

_____

_____

_____

_____

_____

_____

_____

_____

_____

THE UNPARDONABLE SIN

Some people believe that God cannot forgive them. They think they have committed the unpardonable sin.

The Pharisees accused Jesus of doing the works He did by the power of Satan (Matthew 12:24). Jesus replied by stating, in effect, that to attribute to Satan the works of God was unforgivable (Matthew 12:31, 32), and that is essentially the unpardonable sin.

What Scripture Says

"But when the Pharisees heard it, they said, This fellow doth not cast out devils, but by Beelzebub the prince of the devils. . . . Wherefore I say unto you, All manner of sin and blasphemy shall be forgiven unto men: . . . And whosoever speaketh a word against the Son of man, it shall be forgiven him: but whosoever speaketh against the Holy Ghost, it shall not be forgiven him, neither in this world, neither in the world to come" (Matthew 12:24, 31, 32).

"Say ye of him, whom the Father hath sanctified, and sent into the world, Thou blasphemest; because I said, I am the Son of God? If I do not the works of my Father, believe me not. But if I do, though ye believe not me, believe the works: that ye may know, and believe, that the Father is in me, and I in him" (John 10:36-38).

"And I thank Christ Jesus our Lord, who hath enabled me, for that he counted me faithful, putting me into the ministry; Who was before a blasphemer, and a persecutor, and injurious: but I obtained mercy, because I did it ignorantly in unbelief" (1 Timothy 1:12, 13).

Understanding the Unpardonable Sin

It is possible to commit the unpardonable sin, but it must be a very deliberate act. You cannot do so by "accident." The Apostle Paul wrote to Timothy that he, Paul, had been a blasphemer and persecutor of Christ. No doubt he had given the same quick answers as the other Pharisees, that the works of Christ were not those of God. What Paul did or said was not the conscious, willful act of blasphemy of which Jesus spoke, but he "did it ignorantly in unbelief."

A person who has continually, habitually rebelled against God and ignored the Holy Spirit's conviction of sin, righteousness and judgment (John 16:7-11) may finally be given over to having a reprobate mind (Romans 1:18-32). But he must continually be doing evil and reveling in his godlessness. Even then, how can he know that he has reached the point of "no return" where God will no longer strive with him (Genesis 6:3) to bring him to repentance?

God's will is that all should be saved (John 3:16-19). Therefore, He works through everything that you ever experienced to bring you to repentance (Romans 8:28; John 6:44). If you are feeling anxious because you are afraid you may have committed this sin, the very fact of your concern for repentance and forgiveness shows that such anxiety is groundless. A person who blasphemes against the Holy Spirit will not have a desire in his heart to repent, because his behavior is constantly evil (Matthew 12:30, 33-35). Let God's grace calm your troubled heart.

Trust Jesus for forgiveness of sin, whether your sins are resulting in a failing home relationship, an inability to be free from sinful habits, emotional instability or even demonic bondage. Be confident in the ability of Christ to forgive all manner of sin and blasphemy (Matthew 12:31a). By faith, ask Jesus to forgive your sin, to save you, and to receive you into His kingdom as you deliberately commit yourself to Him.

Satan is called the "accuser of the brethren." It is fairly common to be assailed by the thought that the unpardonable sin has somehow been committed. Such great men in the past as Martin Luther and John Bunyan, who wrote *Pilgrim's Progress,* were obsessed with this thought. They came out of their depressions through learning of the rich promises of God and accepting them in faith.

This really is a demonic torment. If you are a Christian, in Jesus' name boldly rebuke the demonic spirit of deception. Then, allow the Holy Spirit to begin putting within you a new, godly nature (Galatians 5:22, 23).

THE UNPARDONABLE SIN

To settle the matter, see your pastor and pray with him that you may be saved by the power of God. Then join in a church fellowship with other Christians where you can continue to grow in Christ.

As You Pray

Thank God for the revelation that the unpardonable sin was not committed. Pray that you will receive God's peace and recommit yourself to the Lord Jesus.

If you still have doubts, ask your pastor to pray, bind and cast out any demonic power in your life. Pray with praise and thanksgiving to God for His Word through which the Holy Spirit bears witness with joy and peace.

References/Homework

Proverbs 3:5, 6	Trust God
1 John 1:9	Sin confessed is forgiven
Matthew 10:24, 25	Expect the same as your teacher receives
1 Corinthians 12:3	The Spirit-led cannot curse Jesus
Ephesians 4:30	God's mark of ownership
Romans 4, 5, 6	Justification by faith

Notes

_____

_____

_____

_____

_____

_____

_____

_____

_____

VENGEANCE

Vengeance is punishment given in retaliation for an injury or offense. It is getting even, taking "an eye for an eye." In addition to the natural urge to be vindictive and get even, in some cultures vengeance is a matter of family duty in which honor of the individual is at stake.

In the Old Testament, the statute of taking "an eye for an eye and a tooth for a tooth" was not a ticket for revenge, but a legal limit to prevent people in anger from going far beyond. The New Testament is extremely clear that believers in Jesus, who have experienced the unmerited forgiveness and love of God, are not to seek vengeance. Good is to overcome evil, forgiveness is to bridge broken relationships, and love (even for an enemy) is to follow the pattern of our Lord and demonstrate to the world the newness of life in Christ (Matthew 5:38-48).

What Scripture Says

"Ye have heard that it hath been said, An eye for an eye, and a tooth for a tooth: But I say unto you, That ye resist not evil: but whosoever shall smite thee on thy right cheek, turn to him the other also. And if any man will sue thee at the law, and take away thy coat, let him have thy cloak also. And whosoever shall compel thee to go a mile, go with him twain. Give to him that asketh thee, and from him that would borrow of thee turn not thou away. Ye have heard that it hath been said, Thou shalt love thy neighbour, and hate thine enemy. But I say unto you, Love your enemies, bless them that curse you, do good to them that hate you, and pray for them which despitefully use you, and persecute you; That ye may be the children of your Father which is in heaven: for he maketh his sun to rise on the evil and on the good, and sendeth rain on the just and on the unjust. For if ye love them which love you, what reward have ye? do not even the publicans the same? And if ye salute your brethren only, what do ye more than others? do not even the publicans so? Be ye therefore perfect, even as your Father which is in heaven is perfect"(Matthew 5:38-48).

"Recompense to no man evil for evil. Provide things honest in the sight of all men. If it be possible, as much as lieth in you, live peaceably with all men. Dearly beloved, avenge not yourselves, but rather give place unto wrath: for it is written, Vengeance is mine; I will repay, saith the Lord. Therefore if thine enemy hunger, feed him; if he thirst, give him drink: for in so doing thou shalt heap coals of fire on his head. Be not overcome of evil, but overcome evil with good" (Romans 12:17-21).

"Let all bitterness, and wrath, and anger, and clamour, and evil speaking, be put away from you, with all malice: And be ye kind one to another, tenderhearted, forgiving one another, even as God for Christ's sake hath forgiven you. Be ye therefore followers of God, as dear children; And walk in love, as Christ also hath loved us, and hath given himself for us an offering and a sacrifice to God for a sweet-smelling savour" (Ephesians 4:31–5:2).

How to Overcome

If some hurt has caused you to want vengeance, explore the hurt openly rather than brooding over it in your heart. God can bring something good out of any experience, hurtful or not (Romans 8:28).

Repent of your own sins, especially of hate and desire for vengeance. Thank God for His love, patience and forgiveness so that you can also forgive.

Ask God to forgive your offender (Mark 11:25). You will be freed from the hurt and desire for vengeance as you pray for and receive a love for him. If you harbor hate and desire vengeance, you will find yourself in spiritual bondage, becoming more bitter, resentful and even physically ill. Hate (sin) has its own wage and will destroy you (Romans 6:23). To forgive is to be set free.

Plan specific actions to encourage reconciliation and love, such as writing a letter, making an apology, or doing kindness in place of vengeance. Where the offense was very personal, such as between husband and wife, you may need very specific help. Your local pastor or a Christian counselor can help, or ask a Christian friend to pray with you to help you overcome your vengefulness.

It is often easy to forgive, but difficult to forget. If vengeance resurfaces in your heart, pray that God will heal the memory of the offense. Also, you can remember an offense with forgiveness, even though it is difficult to forget.

As You Pray

Offer thanks and praise that you are tempted to desire vengeance, through which blessings are coming (Ephesians 5:20; 1 Thessalonians 5:18; Romans 8:28). Thank God for His total forgiveness and un-earned love. Tell Him that you desire to forgive, praying: "Father, in the name of Jesus, I forgive . . . (Name the person or persons who have caused hurt)." Then pray to be filled with the Holy Spirit, and that He will produce within you the fruit of the Spirit to replace bitterness, hate, and desire for vengeance.

References/Homework

Read *The Renewed Mind,* Larry Christenson.

Homework: At each thought of unforgiveness, hatred, etc., confess and repent of it. Jesus died for those sins and they are forgiven when confessed.

Proverbs 6:34	Jealousy repaid by God
Hebrews 10:30	Vengeance is for God
2 Timothy 1:7	Love and self-control replace fear
Galatians 5:23	Fruit of the Holy Spirit

Notes

_____

_____

_____

_____

_____

_____

WITNESSING

Witnessing is telling others about the forgiveness, love, deliverance, empowering, fruitful life and ministry, etc., that you have found in Jesus.

Jesus' last instructions to His disciples before He ascended to His Father were in relation to witnessing. He commissioned them to make disciples as they went into all the world, and to baptize and teach them. He promised them that when they received the Holy Spirit they would be powerful witnesses of Him. The Lord will confirm your witness, just as He did the witness of His apostles with signs following (Mark 16:20; Matthew 18:19, 20).

What Scripture Says

"Go ye therefore, and teach all nations, baptizing them in the name of the Father, and of the Son, and of the Holy Ghost: Teaching them to observe all things whatsoever I have commanded you: and, lo, I am with you alway, even unto the end of the world. Amen" (Matthew 28:19, 20).

"But ye shall receive power, after that the Holy Ghost is come upon you: and ye shall be witnesses unto me both in Jerusalem, and in all Judaea, and in Samaria, and unto the uttermost part of the earth" (Acts 1:8).

"Verily, verily, I say unto you, He that believeth on me, the works that I do shall he do also; and greater works than these shall he do; because I go unto my Father" (John 14:12).

"He [the Holy Spirit] shall glorify me: for he shall receive of mine, and shall shew it unto you" (John 16:14).

Counsel

YOU ARE A WITNESS. When a person has experienced the forgiveness of his sins, he is then able to witness or give testimony to the salvation that is found through Jesus Christ. This does not make you an evangelist, as is mentioned in Ephesians 4:11, but it puts you in the same place as those who were witnesses in the early church. They said, "For we cannot but speak the things which we have seen and heard" (Acts 4:20). You are able to witness about Jesus, for you have met Him personally.

God's desire is that everyone, worldwide, be reconciled to Him, and He has given Christians the "word of reconciliation." That privilege uniquely belongs to all who have believed in Christ (2 Corinthians 5:19).

The authority to witness is from Jesus (Matthew 28:19, 20). The power and boldness to witness is given as a result of the work of the Holy Spirit (Mark 16:17-20; Acts 1:8). The willingness to witness is a decision each one must make. The message to share is the simple truth that "God loves you. Jesus saves all who come to Him in repentance of sin and who have faith in Him. He gives life (John 10:10), equips for living through the Holy Spirit, and He is coming again."

Your own testimony is the best witness you can share. It is not just teaching Bible truths. It is "being" a product of those truths. In other words, don't just say it—be it and do it. Allow the Holy Spirit to produce within you the fruit of the Spirit: love, joy, peace, meekness, goodness, kindness, faithfulness, patience, and self-control, thereby "becoming" what you are witnessing to.

As You Pray

Pray that God will fill you with the Holy Spirit, equipping you for witnessing. You may have to pray to be released from bondages of fear or feelings of not knowing enough or not being good enough to share Jesus with others. The general direction of prayer should be that you want to be bold and free to share your faith with whomever may be open to your witness during your daily life.

Ask God each morning to lead you to someone to whom you can witness. Expect Him to do so. As you read God's Word, ask Him to give you a message that day for someone who needs your witness.

WITNESSING

References/Homework

Psalm 14:3; Ecclesiastes 7:20	The guilt of man
Romans 5:10; James 4:4; Colossians 1:21	Separation from God
2 Thessalonians 1:8, 9; 2 Peter 3:7	God's judgment upon the ungodly
1 Timothy 2:5; Hebrews 12:24; John 4:16; Acts 4:12	God's provision for man
Ephesians 4:32; 1 John 2:12; Acts 5:31; 13:38; 26:18	Forgiveness
Isaiah 1:18; 1 John 1:7; Revelation 7:14	Cleansing
Acts 13:39; Romans 3:24; 8:30; Titus 3:7	Justification
Ephesians 2:8, 9; Titus 2:11; 3:4-7; Romans 3:34	By grace
John 15	Stay in Jesus
1 Corinthians 13	Witness in love

Acquire a *Christian Worker's New Testament.*

Notes

_____

_____

_____

_____

_____

_____